USBORNE BOOK OF

ATHLETICS

Paula Woods
Edited by Susan Peach
Designed by Chris Scollen

Athletics Consultant: Frank Dick
(Director of coaching, British Amateur Athletic Board)

Illustrated by:
Paul Wilding, Guy Smith and Chris Lyon
Cover illustration by Gordon Lawson

All photographs courtesy of All-Sport UK
Commissioned photographs taken by Bob Martin

With thanks to Ian Down, Ian Winter and Lillywhites Cantabrian Ltd.

Contents

First published in 1988 by Usborne Publishing Ltd, 20 Garrick Street, London WC2E 9BJ, England. Copyright ©1988 Usborne Publishing Ltd. **American edition 1988.** Printed in Great Britain

The origins of athletics

Athletics is a collection of separate sports, which over the centuries have come to take place within the same arena. In ancient times sport was primarily seen as a means of training for warfare, and the actual term athletics is derived from the Greek word *Athlos*, which means a fight, competition or combat.

Throwing events

Throwing events such as the javelin and discus formed part of the Ancient Greek games which date from 776 BC. These games were held every four years in Olympia, until around AD 393. The javelin was orginally a weapon, whilst the discus is said to have been adapted from the round flat shields carried by soldiers.

The hammer and shot are Celtic in origin. It is thought that they were first introduced at the Scottish Highland games during the fourteenth century. At these games, athletes threw sledge hammers and large stones.

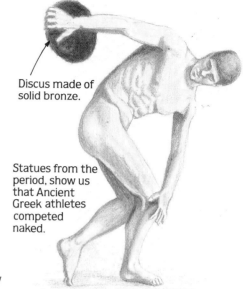

Discus made of solid bronze.

Statues from the period, show us that Ancient Greek athletes competed naked.

Jumping events

The only jumping event to be included in the Ancient Greek games was the long jump. Unlike the long jump of today, however, athletes carried weights which they discarded on take-off.

The pole vault, high jump and triple jump all originate from the Scottish Highland games. The pole vault was originally used in rural districts to clear walls and ditches. When it was first introduced as a sporting event, the pole was fitted with a large spike which competitors would plant firmly in the ground when vaulting.

Running events

Some running events can be traced back to the Ancient Greek games. The three main events were the *stade* (192m sprint), the *diaulos* (192m and back) and the *dolichos* (around 5,000m).

Hurdling and steeplechase, however, are more likely to have originated in Britain at rural sports meetings, during the nineteenth century. The hurdles were heavy sheep gates embedded in the ground. As athletes could injure themselves if they hit one, they were forced to adopt a much higher jumping action than that seen today.

The steeplechase, so-called because it was originally run between two church steeples, was for many years seen as a comic event. Huge water jumps were constructed as part of the course, so that athletes would inevitably fall in, to the amusement of the spectators.

The first official steeplechase was in 1864, at a university meeting between Oxford and Cambridge.

Points to remember

■ All athletic events are now measured by the metric system. However, for those more used to the imperial system there is a conversion chart on page 47.

■ In athletics, times are always written as hours, then minutes and seconds. For example, 1:2.33 mins is 1 hour, 2 minutes and 33 seconds.

■ Where they first appear in a section, technical terms are printed in *italics* and explained in the glossary on pages 46-47.

■ Each event is accompanied by a guide to top performances. These indicate the height, distance or time athletes must achieve if they are to be amongst the top twenty in the world.

3

The stadium

An athletics stadium is arranged so that both track (running) and field (jumping and throwing) events may be staged simultaneously. As a result a large number of officials are required to keep events running smoothly and spectators and competitors informed. Below you can find out about the layout of the stadium, the functions of the major officials and the sophisticated equipment they use.

The track

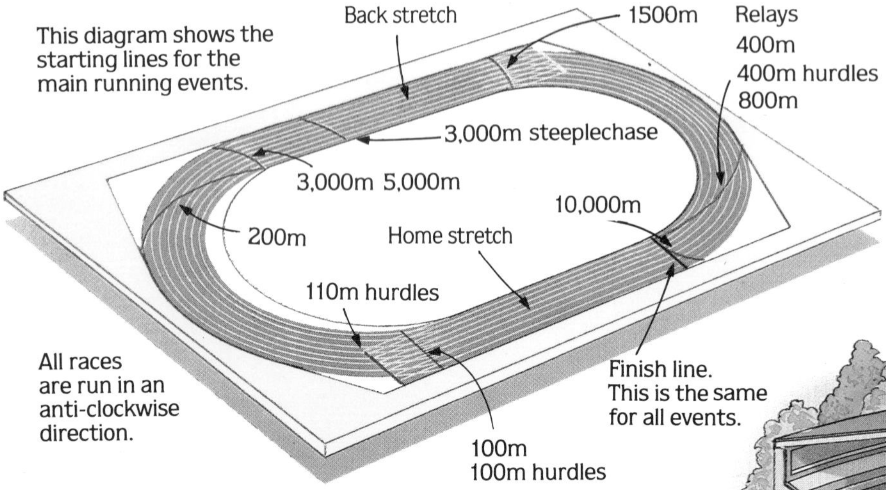

This diagram shows the starting lines for the main running events.

Back stretch

1500m

Relays
400m
400m hurdles
800m

3,000m steeplechase

3,000m 5,000m

10,000m

200m

Home stretch

110m hurdles

Finish line.
This is the same for all events.

100m
100m hurdles

All races are run in an anti-clockwise direction.

All stadiums now have artificial track surfaces and runways, usually made of plastic or rubber. These have the advantage of being both weather-resistant and hard-wearing. One complete circuit measures 400m. For major events the track is divided into eight lanes all of which measure at least 1.22m in width. These lanes are always numbered from the inside edge, outwards.

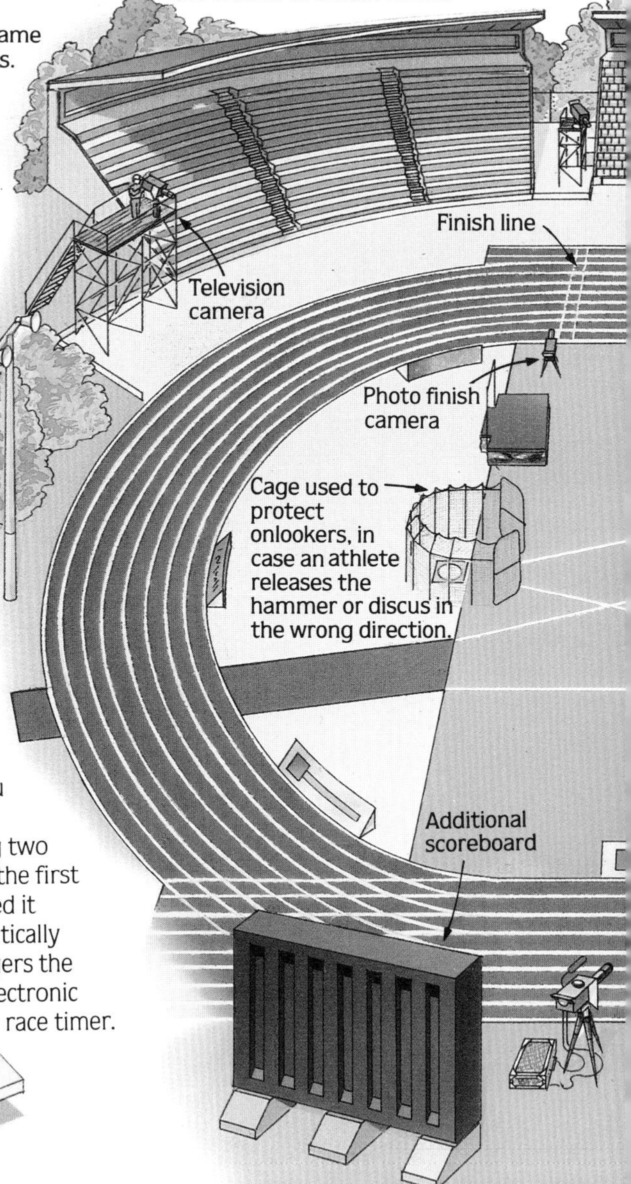

The infield

The majority of field events take place in the centre of the track (the *infield*). The exceptions to this are the long jump, triple jump and pole vault which may be situated outside the track (as shown below). The size and shape of event areas are always the same, but their position will depend on individual stadiums.

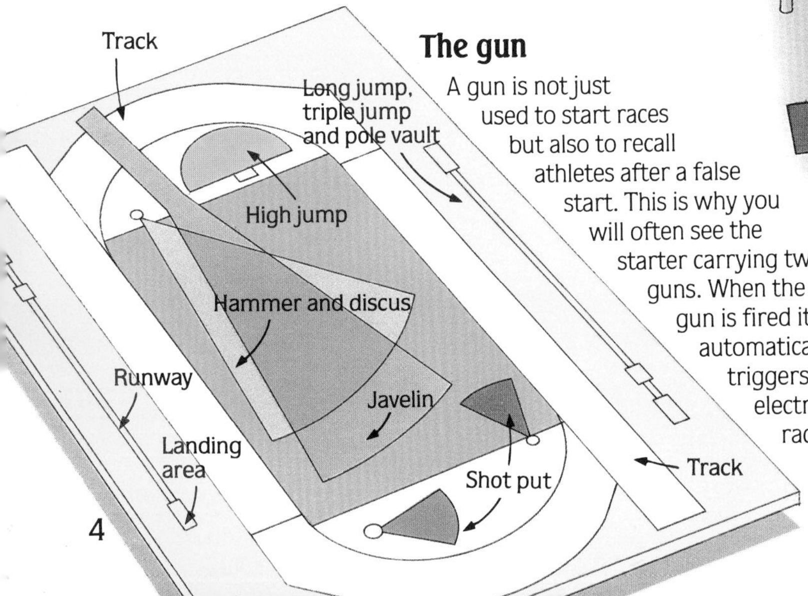

Track

Long jump, triple jump and pole vault

High jump

Hammer and discus

Runway

Javelin

Landing area

Shot put

Track

The gun

A gun is not just used to start races but also to recall athletes after a false start. This is why you will often see the starter carrying two guns. When the first gun is fired it automatically triggers the electronic race timer.

Photo finishes

Accuracy is essential when measuring athletes' times. This is achieved by means of a sophisticated camera which is focused on the finish line. The camera records the image of each athlete crossing the line and also inscribes the individual finishing times on the film. This equipment is capable of measuring times to within a thousandth of a second and is especially useful in establishing the winner in a close finish.

Television camera

Finish line

Photo finish camera

Cage used to protect onlookers, in case an athlete releases the hammer or discus in the wrong direction.

Additional scoreboard

Wind gauge

Strong winds often affect performances for better or worse. When aiding sprinters and jumpers to better times and distances the performances are said to be *wind assisted*. A world record cannot be set if the wind is stronger than 2m per second, or 4m per second for the decathlon and heptathlon.

You can see wind gauges alongside the track close to the inside lane and alongside the jump runway 20m from the take-off board. The gauge is placed parallel to the runway or track. As each athlete performs, the windspeed is automatically measured and the result displayed on a digital readout.

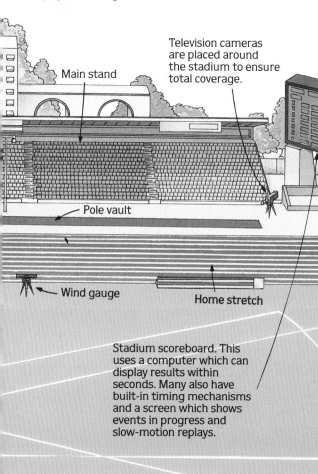

Main stand

Television cameras are placed around the stadium to ensure total coverage.

Pole vault

Wind gauge

Home stretch

Stadium scoreboard. This uses a computer which can display results within seconds. Many also have built-in timing mechanisms and a screen which shows events in progress and slow-motion replays.

Mobile field event scoreboards. These show the athlete's number, the number of attempts made, whether the current trial was valid and, if so, the height and distance achieved.

Back stretch

Wind gauge

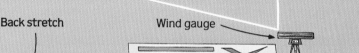

Landing area

Runway for long jump and triple jump.

Sprinting

There are three major sprint events: the 100m, 200m and 400m, outlined on pages 8-9. All these involve athletes running at top speed throughout the race. Athletes must stay within their designated lanes.

While there is no ideal physique for sprinters, you may notice that they are often tall and long-legged. In order to be successful they require a combination of leg speed, fast reactions and strength. This is often referred to as *explosive power*.

■ Not all runners have the classic sprinter's build of Carl Lewis (1053). Ben Johnson (145), seen here breaking the world record in 1987, is far more compact and relies on muscle power and fast reflexes.

Starting the race

Before bringing the athletes under starter's orders, the starter must first position himself so that he can see all the runners clearly. The starter will stand alongside or behind the runners depending on whether the race has a *staggered* or *straight start* (see right). The three start commands are then given.

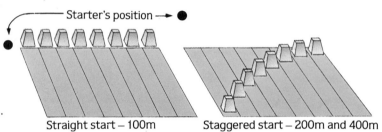

Straight start – 100m   Staggered start – 200m and 400m

1 On your marks

On hearing this command the athlete moves to the blocks and, using his hands for support, backs into them. The balls of his feet are firmly placed against the blocks, with his toes usually resting on the track for support. His hands must be behind the *scratch line* (starting line). He does not lay the palms of his hands on the track, but uses his fingers and thumbs to form a bridge. His arms should be straight as this helps him to maintain a stable position in the blocks.

Shoulders in line with hands.

Feet pressed firmly against the blocks.

Arms straight

Hands behind line

2 Set

The athlete raises his hips and tips his body forward so that his shoulders are now in front of his hands. He looks directly down at the track below; looking up would cause the athlete to lower his hips, resulting in a bad start. The starter holds the athletes in this position for an average of two seconds before the gun is fired.

Hips are higher than the shoulders.

3 Fire

On hearing the gun, the athlete removes his hands from the ground and drives his front leg hard against the block whilst moving his rear leg forward. His arms pump quickly back and forth.

The athlete should run smoothly out of the blocks with his body low. He will then rise gradually until he has reached full stride length.

Body low

Leg drives hard against the blocks.

Technique

The athlete's first stride out of the blocks is around one metre in length. Each subsequent step should increase until a natural stride length of around two metres is reached. A good sprinter will only take around seven or eight strides to reach his natural length.

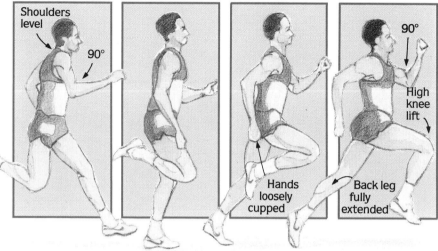

Shoulders level

90°

90°

High knee lift

Hands loosely cupped

Back leg fully extended

Having reached his natural stride, the athlete's run should appear as one smooth continuous motion. As these pictures show, his shoulders should be level, with no tension apparent in his neck or face. His arms pump back and forth, reaching back to his hip and forward to his shoulder. To avoid tension in his arms, the athlete loosely cups his hands.

The sprinter's stride should be long, with the driving leg fully extended behind to push him forward. He tucks the other foot up under his buttock before pulling the leg forward into a high knee lift.

Any sideways movement, such as shoulders moving from side to side or feet pointing outwards, is a sign of bad technique.

The finish

At the finish, the winner is the athlete whose torso (trunk) crosses the finish line first.

In her attempt to beat opponents, the runner thrusts her chest forward in the final stride, throwing her arms back behind her body. This helps to push her forward, and is often referred to as a *dip finish*.

The athlete must time her dip finish perfectly. Dipping too soon means that she will decelerate rapidly as her arms are no longer pumping. However, a well-timed dip finish can mean the difference between an athlete winning and losing the race.

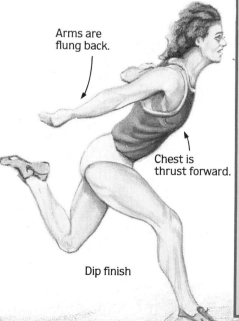

Arms are flung back.

Chest is thrust forward.

Dip finish

Equipment

Starting blocks

Foot plates can be moved back and forth and their angle adjusted.

Sensory mechanism

Blocks are used in all sprint and hurdle events as they give the athlete a solid base from which to push off. They consist of a metal bar with a pair of adjustable, angled foot plates attached. The blocks are nailed to the track just behind the scratch line. They also have a built-in sensory mechanism which detects whether a foot has left the blocks within 0.1 seconds of the gun. This counts as a *false start* and triggers a light on top of an indicator box. Any runner who makes or causes two false starts is disqualified.

Shoes

Sprinting shoes are very light and only weigh around 160-210g whereas ordinary trainers weigh around 320g. They provide little support for the heels as sprinters run on the balls of their feet.

Element

No heel as this would add weight to the shoe.

Six removable spikes are fitted at the front of the shoe. These help the sprinter grip the track, and can be replaced when worn or damaged.

Spikes, however, dig into the track surface which causes the athlete to use up extra energy. Blunt spikes, called *elements*, are now available which, while providing a grip, do not dig into the surface.

100 metres

The 100m takes place on the home straight (see page 4) and is probably the most prestigious of all the sprint events. At this distance it is particularly important that the athlete starts well and gets into his full stride as quickly as possible. Any hesitation at the gun could lose an athlete the race, as there is no time to rectify mistakes.

Here you can see how the 100m can be broken into three distinct stages.

1. Driving strides (20-30m)

2. Acceleration (30-60m)

3. Maintaining speed (60m onwards)

1. Driving strides as the athlete pushes forward.

20-30m

Start

Surprisingly, when an athlete appears to be speeding up in the final stage, he is actually decelerating at a slower rate than his opponents.

60m +

3. To try to avoid slowing down, the athlete attempts to relax and maintain good style, while increasing arm and leg movement.

Finish

2. Most athletes reach top speed at around 60m. After this they may begin to tire and slow down.

30-60m
Acceleration to top speed.

200 metres

As the 200m begins on a bend (see page 4), a *staggered start* is required to ensure that each athlete runs the same distance.

In the 200m the acceleration stage is slightly less furious than the 100m as athletes must retain energy for a longer race. They will therefore reach a slightly lower maximum speed.

The blocks are placed towards the outer limit of the lane.

Athletes set their blocks at an angle to the bend so that their first strides may be run in a straight line.

■ When running the bend at top speed athletes are thrown towards the outside edge of the lane, increasing the distance they have to run. To overcome this they lean into the bend, as shown in the photograph, and drop their inside arm while bringing the other slightly across their body.

As the athletes arrive at the end of the bend their true race positions are revealed. They will then consciously attempt to accelerate and maintain their speed by vigorously moving their arms and legs. Top class sprinters tend to run the second half of the race faster than the first. This is because athletes cannot reach top speed on the bend and the second 100m benefits from them being already on the move (a *flying start*).

Training

The best sprinters in the world are capable of running faster than 40km per hour. This speed is achieved by contracting and relaxing the muscles extremely rapidly.

Muscles are made up of two different fibres:

★ Slow twitch fibres allow steady work over a prolonged period by converting oxygen to energy. This is called the *aerobic system*.

★ Fast twitch fibres provide immediate energy over short periods and, as they store a form of fuel called ATP, do not use oxygen. This is called the *anaerobic system*.

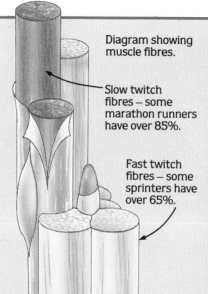

Diagram showing muscle fibres.

Slow twitch fibres – some marathon runners have over 85%.

Fast twitch fibres – some sprinters have over 65%.

It is the fast twitch fibres that the athlete uses when sprinting, as they are capable of contracting in 0.04-0.09 seconds.

In training, sprinters aim to improve this contraction rate along with their *explosive power*, endurance, and technique. Training places emphasis on bounding (high springing runs), weight training, suppleness and technique drills. As 200m and 400m runners require more speed endurance than 100m runners their training is more rigorous. They will carry out the same work but over longer periods of time and distances.

400 metres

This is the longest and most demanding of the sprints, requiring both stamina and speed. The athlete must pace himself carefully and balance his effort between the two halves of the race. The second half should be no more than one or two seconds slower than the first.

The acceleration stage is not as explosive as in the 100m and 200m, as in order to save energy the runner increases his effort gradually. He does not reach maximum speed until around 150-200m. The runner may start to experience fatigue at 200m. This becomes more pronounced as he enters the *home stretch*. He must now concentrate on staying relaxed and ensuring good running technique. This helps him maintain speed through to the finish.

The bends can also cause problems: athletes in the inside lanes must negotiate very tight bends, whilst those in the outside lanes cannot see their opponents.

Diagram showing the stages of a 400m race.

At 200m fatigue begins.

Inside lanes have disadvantage of a tight bend.

At 300m positions are clear, and fatigue becomes pain.

Staggered start

Finish

Lanes 3-7 have advantage of a gentle bend. Athletes can also see opponents.

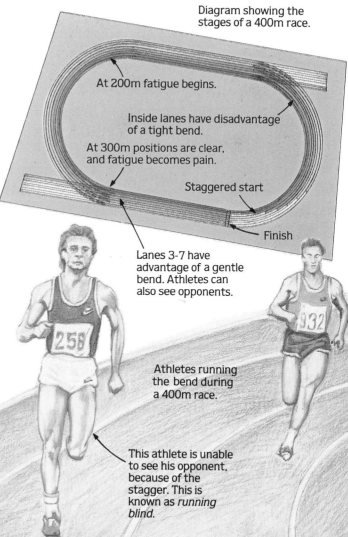

Athletes running the bend during a 400m race.

This athlete is unable to see his opponent, because of the stagger. This is known as *running blind*.

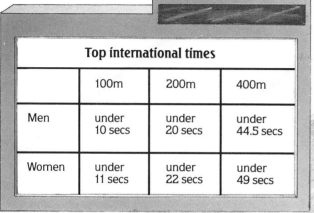

Top international times			
	100m	200m	400m
Men	under 10 secs	under 20 secs	under 44.5 secs
Women	under 11 secs	under 22 secs	under 49 secs

Relays

The 4 x 100m and 4 x 400m relays are often seen as the highlight of major competitions such as the Olympics, and are traditionally the last events of the meet. The relay is a team event. There are four members in a team and they each run part of the total distance (known as a *leg*). The first runner carries a baton which is then handed on from one member of the team to another.

The change-over zone

The passing of the baton (the *change-over*) must be carried out within a specific 20m zone. This is marked on the track in yellow for the 4 x 100m and blue for the 4 x 400m. If the baton is not passed within this zone the team is disqualified. In the 4 x 100m, the outgoing runner (the runner receiving the baton) is allowed to start running 10m before the change-over zone, in order to build up speed.

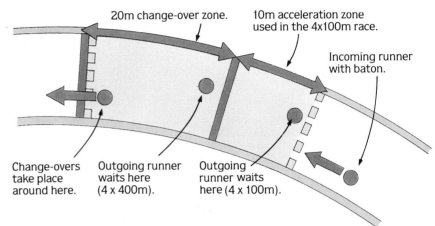

20m change-over zone.

10m acceleration zone used in the 4x100m race.

Incoming runner with baton.

Change-overs take place around here.

Outgoing runner waits here (4 x 400m).

Outgoing runner waits here (4 x 100m).

4 x 100m

This race consists of one complete circuit of the track. It is vital that runners do not slow down during the change-overs, as they will not be able to make up any lost time. The baton is therefore passed with both athletes running at full speed.

A good change-over will take place in the final 10m of the zone, at which point the outgoing runner should be running at the same speed as her team-mate. In training, the two runners work out which point the incoming runner should reach when the outgoing runner starts to run. They are allowed to mark this point on the track, usually with

sticky tape. This is called a *checkmark*.

In the 4x100m race, runners use a *non-visual change-over*. This means that the outgoing runner does not look back at the incoming runner when the baton is passed. The baton can be passed by either the *upsweep* or *downsweep* method, shown on the opposite page. If the baton is dropped, the team is not disqualified as long as the runner who dropped it also retrieves it.

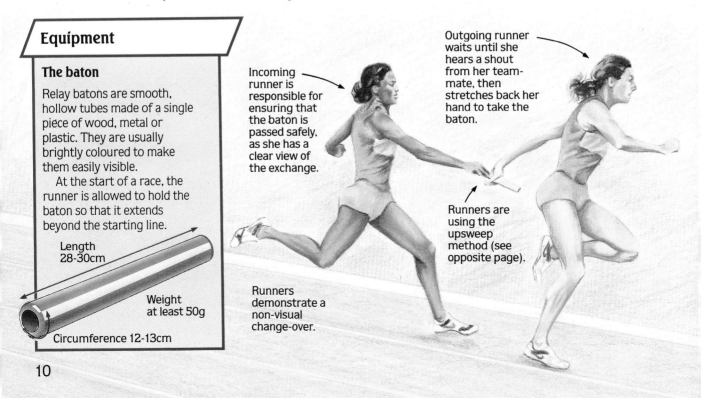

Equipment

The baton

Relay batons are smooth, hollow tubes made of a single piece of wood, metal or plastic. They are usually brightly coloured to make them easily visible.

At the start of a race, the runner is allowed to hold the baton so that it extends beyond the starting line.

Length 28-30cm

Weight at least 50g

Circumference 12-13cm

Incoming runner is responsible for ensuring that the baton is passed safely, as she has a clear view of the exchange.

Outgoing runner waits until she hears a shout from her team-mate, then stretches back her hand to take the baton.

Runners are using the upsweep method (see opposite page).

Runners demonstrate a non-visual change-over.

The downsweep

The outgoing runner stretches her arm out behind her with the palm of her hand facing upwards. The incoming runner brings the baton down into the "V" of the receiver's hand.

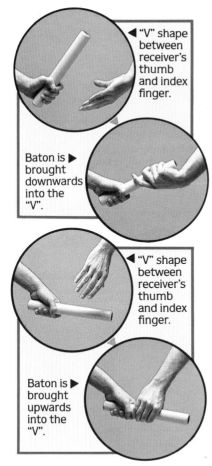

◀ "V" shape between receiver's thumb and index finger.

Baton is ▶ brought downwards into the "V".

The upsweep

The outgoing runner reaches backwards with her arm bent at the elbow and her hand pointing downwards. The incoming runner brings the baton upwards into the "V" of the receiver's hand.

◀ "V" shape between receiver's thumb and index finger.

Baton is ▶ brought upwards into the "V".

The passing sequence

In the 4 x 100m relay, the baton is passed from one runner's right hand into the next runner's left hand, then from the left hand to the right and so on. Athletes keep the baton in their receiving hand, as transferring it from one hand to the other would waste time.

The first and third runners (who run the bends) carry the baton in their right hands, so that they can keep to the inside of their lane and be in the correct position to pass the baton to the next runner.

Running order in the 4x100m

The running order should take into account the particular strengths of each athlete. For example, the lead (first) runner must be a good starter and bend runner. As the second and third legs are the longest (over 120m, as the runner must cover two change-over zones) these runners are often 200m specialists. The final runner has to be a good finisher.

4 x 400m

This race consists of four circuits of the track. As the initial 500m is run in lanes, the first change-over zones are *staggered*. On the second leg, athletes can break from lanes at the end of the first bend. The zone for the second and third change-overs is situated 10m to either side of the finish line, and is marked by flags.

Passing technique

As each 400m leg is so tiring, the incoming runner's judgement may be impaired by fatigue. The outgoing runner therefore uses a *visual change-over*, in which he looks back when the baton is passed. Although this is safer and easier than the non-visual exchange, it is slower.

■ Outgoing runners have to make space for the change-over by holding off their opponents with their arms and bottoms.

The outgoing runner turns to watch his team-mate, so that he can judge when to run. He should match his team-mate's speed, so that they can transfer the baton in the final 10m of the change-over zone. The athletes are bunched together during the final two change-overs and must jostle for position (see photograph).

The passing sequence

Most athletes prefer to run with the baton in their right hand. The receiver therefore takes the baton in his left hand and quickly transfers it to his right hand, ready to pass to the next runner's left hand.

Running order in the 4x400m

As the first leg is run in lanes it is a good place to put the least experienced runner of the team. The second and third runners have to be quite aggressive, as they often have to jostle for position in the change-over zones.

The runner on the final leg is invariably the strongest in the team in order to make up any lost ground or maintain a lead.

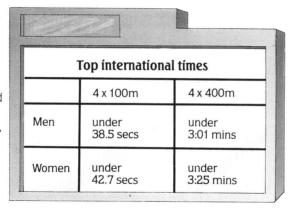

Top international times		
	4 x 100m	4 x 400m
Men	under 38.5 secs	under 3:01 mins
Women	under 42.7 secs	under 3:25 mins

Middle distance events

There are two main middle distance events: the 800m and the 1500m. The mile is also classified as a middle distance race, although it is not included in many major championships. Success in these races depends on high speed and good pacing, and athletes require a combination of speed, strength and stamina. They are usually tall and long-legged. Although muscular, they must also be light, as carrying excess weight wastes energy.

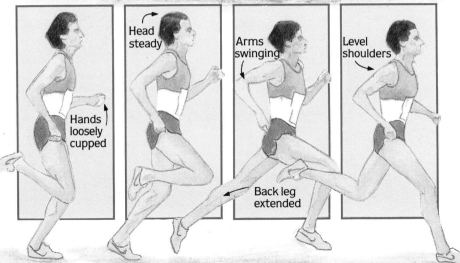

Runners in position for a standing start.

Weight on front leg.

Feet must be behind the starting line.

The start

In the 800m, the start is *staggered* and situated on a bend. The first 100m of this race is run in lanes.* In the 1500m athletes simply line up across the track for the start and can break for the inside lane straight away.

In all middle distance races a standing start is used. There is just one starting command (On your marks) before the gun is fired. On hearing this command, runners adopt a standing start.

Technique

The aim of the middle distance runner is to run the race at a fast and steady pace. His running action is much more economical than a sprinter's because of the extra distance he has to cover during the race.

The athlete moves his arms in a much less exaggerated style than the sprinter's pumping action, and his forearms swing slightly across his body. His stride is also shorter and more relaxed than the sprinter's, and his knee lift is slightly lower. His shoulders should be level, not hunched, as this will cramp his rib cage and, in turn, his lungs. The athlete should keep his hands loosely cupped in order to avoid any tension in his arms.

Hands loosely cupped

Head steady

Arms swinging

Back leg extended

Level shoulders

The athlete's running action is shown above. It should appear effortless, with a rhythmic, bouncy stride. Any sideways movement (such as his head wobbling or shoulder rocking) is a sign of bad technique and restricts his forward drive.

Training

The human body has two systems for generating energy: the *aerobic system* which uses oxygen, and the *anaerobic system*, which does not (see page 9). The anaerobic system provides energy instantly, but only for a short period of time. It is most important in short, fast, explosive events such as sprinting and hurdling. The aerobic system provides long-term energy, but slowly, and is most important in the longer, endurance events such as the marathon.

Middle distance runners have to use both systems simultaneously, as they run too fast and too far for one system alone. Training therefore concentrates on improving both systems. This includes drills such as *interval training* (alternating fast runs and jogs on the track), *resistance work* (for example, running with weights) and strength work. Speed drills are also important, as they help to increase the speed at which an athlete can comfortably cruise.

* The point at which athletes can leave their lanes is marked by red flags and a green line.

Tactics

The athlete's aim is to maintain the same pace throughout the race, as constant changes of speed waste energy. The only variants to the pace should be at the start and finish, when an athlete may have to sprint in order to get into a good position.

Athletes also try to run in the inside lane for as much of the race as possible, as by running in other lanes they have to travel further. By running just one bend in the second lane an athlete has to cover about 4m extra, which uses valuable energy.

Athletes who started the race in the outside lanes try to reach the inside lanes as quickly as possible.

Athletes normally overtake on the outside, as runner 1080 is doing. Although they can pass on the inside they may be disqualified if they jostle another runner.

Runner 840 is ideally positioned behind his opponent's right shoulder. He can overtake at any time by simply running straight ahead, and does not have to wait for a gap.

Runners at the back must not lose contact with the main group, as in middle distance there is little time to make up lost ground.

An athlete is *boxed in* when he is trapped in the inside lane by runners immediately in front and to the side of him.

The runner in the red shirt is boxed in. There is little he can do except wait for a gap to occur so that he can accelerate away.

Race positioning

An athlete has to choose whether to lead the field or follow a leader. In following, he has the advantage of being able to watch the other competitors and make a sudden attack. However, he does run the risk of being boxed in or having to adjust his stride to that of the leaders.

Although the leader has the advantage of dictating the pace and is free to run at his natural stride length, he is unable to see any tactical movements within the field. Some leaders impose a fast early pace in order to tire any fast finishers, who might otherwise overtake them in the final stages.

At the start of the final lap, a bell is rung. This is generally a signal for the pace to increase, as athletes try to break away from the field. This may result in a mass sprint down the *home stretch*.

Pacemakers

During a race where a record is expected you may hear the commentator refer to the *pacemaker*. This is an athlete who has been entered in the race specifically to set the pace in the early laps. He will know exactly how fast he has to run to enable the challenger to break the record. The pacemaker often drops out before the end of the race due to fatigue, as he may have had to run two or three laps at his maximum speed.

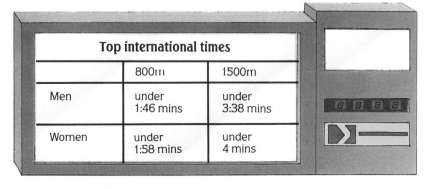

Top international times		
	800m	1500m
Men	under 1:46 mins	under 3:38 mins
Women	under 1:58 mins	under 4 mins

Equipment

Shoes

Shoes for middle distance runners are designed with their technique in mind. Whereas sprinters run constantly on the balls of the feet, middle distance runners will fall on to their heel to cushion the foot against its heavy work load. Their shoes therefore have a strong protective heel wedge.

Wedge

Spike

Long distance events

The long distance track events are the 3,000m (7.5 laps), which is for women only, the 5,000m (12.5 laps) and the 10,000m (25 laps).

In addition to the distance they cover in races, long distance runners may run over 300km per week in training. They therefore possess great reserves of stamina and tend to be very lean as carrying any excess body fat would waste energy.

The start

All long distance races begin with a standing start. As these races start on a bend, athletes line up along a curved start line. Both the 3,000m and 5,000m start at the 200m mark, while the 10,000m start is situated at the beginning of the first bend (see page 4).

Technique

Long distance technique is very similar to that of a middle distance runner, as the athlete's aim is to achieve a constant, steady pace. The running action, however, is once again modified so as to avoid using any unnecessary energy. The athlete's action is now far gentler, with both arm and leg movement reduced.

Tactics

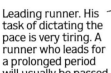

Leading runner. His task of dictating the pace is very tiring. A runner who leads for a prolonged period will usually be passed by fresher runners in the final stages of the race.

Runner tucked in behind the leader's shoulder faces air-resistance reduced by 64%, thus saving a lot of energy.

Athletes often run one behind the other in order to stay in the inside lane and avoid covering extra distance.

Front group of runners breaking away from the rest of the field.

These runners are losing contact with the leading group.

Athletes normally run a brisk first lap as they attempt to gain a good position within the field. The pace then settles down to a more or less constant speed, with runners spread over a distance of about 20m. In the early stages it is not vital for a runner to stay close to the leader, as there is time to make up any lost ground later in the race.

As a race progresses, a number of runners will take it in turns to lead the pack. It is very rare for only one athlete to lead throughout because it is so tiring.

As early as the half-way mark, the strongest runners will start to break away in a leading group. Those athletes who fall behind will eventually be *lapped* (passed by the leaders). You will normally see these runners move out in order to let the leaders run by.

Towards the end of the race, a runner in the leading group may try to throw off his opponents by employing tactics to sap their remaining strength. Some common methods used to do this are described on the opposite page.

Equipment

Lap indicator board

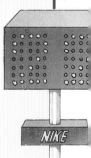

In long distance races, a lap indicator board is placed near the finish line. Athletes may lose count of how many laps they have run, and rely on the lap indicator to show them how many laps remain.

Surging

A front runner may try to *break* (tire) her opponents by applying the pressure of a sustained fast pace or of intermittant bursts of fast pace. The latter is called *surging*. For example, an athlete might run at a steady pace, then increase her speed for about 200m, before returning to her original pace. She would repeat this pattern of fast and slow pace over several laps to establish a comfortable lead (see photograph on right).

Alternatively, she might run at a faster speed until she has gained a lead of 20-30m. Then she would run several laps one or two seconds faster than the previous race pace. This should build up a large enough lead for her to run the rest at race pace.

Surging disrupts other runners' rhythm and concentration and tires them quickly. However, it uses a lot of energy, and an athlete should only attempt to do it if she has carried out proper training (see below).

Winding up the pace

This tactic involves an athlete getting into the lead, then gradually increasing the pace every 100m or 200m This puts pressure on the other runners, who have to use all their energy to keep up with the leader, leaving nothing for the sprint finish.

■ Ingrid Kristiansen winning the 10,000m at the 1986 European Championships. She has built up a considerable lead by setting a sustained fast pace, and her opponents have no energy left for a sprint finish.

Training

In order to perform well, a long distance athlete needs a slow, constant supply of energy. Her muscles have to be fed with large amounts of oxygen, while her muscle fibres must be efficient at using this supply*. In long distance races about 80-90% of the athlete's energy is supplied by the *aerobic system* (see page 9).

In order to improve the efficiency of this system, the athlete carries out rigorous training routines. The bulk of her time is taken up with continuous runs and *fartlek training*. This normally takes place in a park or the countryside, and consists of the athlete running at different speeds according to the terrain. This entails frequent changes of pace, and is therefore good training for surging. Athletes also carry out *alternating runs*, in which they alternate between a fast pace for 1,000m, then a slower pace for 500m.

Mixed in with this is hill and sand dune running, which helps to strengthen their legs, along with track work and speed drills. The athlete will also use *circuit training* to increase her overall strength.

Lap times

Lap times are usually announced, either after each lap or at the end of each kilometre (2.5 laps). An average lap time for men is around 64 seconds in the 5,000m, and around 66 seconds in the 10,000m. Women average around 69 seconds per lap in the 3,000m, and about 10 seconds slower per lap than men in the 5,000m and 10,000m. If the lap times are consistently under these average times, there is a good chance that a record time may be set.

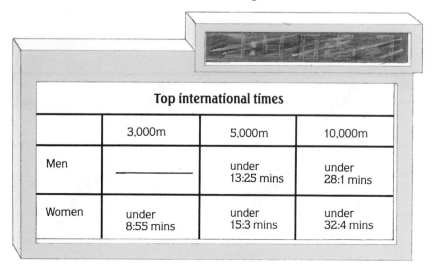

	3,000m	5,000m	10,000m
Top international times			
Men	———	under 13:25 mins	under 28:1 mins
Women	under 8:55 mins	under 15:3 mins	under 32:4 mins

*You can find out more about muscle fibres on page 9.

Marathon

The marathon race is 42.195km (26.2 miles) long. This rather strange distance was first set at the 1908 Olympic Games in London, as the organizers wanted the race to finish in front of the royal box.

The marathon usually takes place around a town or city and, in the case of major championships, such as the Olympics, must start and finish inside a stadium.

Despite its gruelling nature, this event has become increasingly popular with runners of all standards. It is particularly popular with older runners who, although they no longer have sprinting speed, still possess lots of strength and stamina.

The start

In popular events such as the New York or London marathons, there may be several thousand runners lining up at the start.

In these conditions, it may seem advantageous for an athlete to be in the front row, but in fact many prefer to stay further back. This is because it prevents them from being tempted to run off at top speed.

It is vital that a runner settles into his race pace as soon as possible, as if he runs the first few kilometres too fast he will pay for it later.

■ At the start many runners position themselves within a group so that their pace is then regulated by other runners over the first few kilometres.

Diet

In order to increase their supply of energy, runners often go on a special diet before a race. Their main source of energy is glycogen*, which is stored in the muscles. However, there is a point during any marathon (around 29-35km) when this fuel runs out. The body then has to switch to using fat to provide energy. This transition can be very painful and slows the runner down in the last few kilometres. This is referred to as *hitting the wall*.

A runner can delay this process by increasing his supply of glycogen through his diet. Seven days prior to the race he cuts down his intake of carbohydrates (pasta, potatoes and so on), which the body converts to glycogen. After three days he then loads up with carbohydrates. His muscles will try to compensate for the initial loss by storing extra glycogen, thus providing him with more fuel during the race.

Technique

To conserve energy, the marathon runner modifies the technique of the long distance runner, using shorter and less pronounced strides.

The athlete can also save valuable energy by pacing himself evenly. A top marathon runner can run at an average pace of under 3 minutes, 15 seconds per kilometre throughout the entire race.

The form in which the body stores carbohydrates.

Tactics

The tactics used by marathon runners depend on their strengths and weaknesses and those of their opponents, the nature of the course and the weather. Before the race they study a map or drive round the course, looking for any hazards, such as hills or cobbles. They should also obtain a weather forecast as very hot or windy weather will force them to run at a slower pace. Many athletes create a race plan based on these factors in order to pace themselves.

Runners' tactics vary enormously. One athlete might run a fast, even pace throughout the race in the hope of outrunning his opponents. Another might bide his time and make a late or strategic break. Many wait and try to whittle down the leading group either by a series of *surges**, or by *winding up the pace** in the final stages.

Runners participating in the New York marathon.

The televising of the New York marathon encouraged many people to take up running, and sparked the marathon boom of the 1970s.

In many marathons a large leading group will stay together until near the end of the race.

Ultra distance

An ultra distance race is any race longer than a marathon. One of the longest was the Trans–America race from New York to Los Angeles. It was some 5,897km long and took the winner 79 days to complete (an average of 74km per day). Another variation is the six day race, in which runners attempt to cover as much distance as possible during this period.

Training

Marathon runners need an enormous weekly mileage to build up stamina. Top runners train for an average of 120-190km each week. As well as continuous running on roads, they use *fartlek* (see page 15) and *interval training* on the track.

In the week before a race, athletes reduce their training as at this point they should be at peak performance and do not want to tire themselves unnecessarily.

Top international times	
Men	around 2:10.12 hrs
Women	around 2:24.28 hrs

* These tactics can be found on page 15.

Equipment

Shoes

The constant jarring action of running on a hard surface can cause serious injuries to athletes' feet and legs. Their shoes therefore need to cushion and support their feet, especially under the heel. They must be lightweight and fit perfectly, as any friction will cause painful blisters. Marathon shoes have rubber soles and are not fitted with spikes.

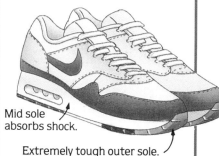

Mid sole absorbs shock.

Extremely tough outer sole.

Refreshments

It is easy for marathon runners to become overheated or dehydrated during a race, especially on a hot day when they lose a lot of fluid in sweat. To prevent this, they need to drink plenty of liquids during the race. However, even this will not prevent them sweating away several pounds of body weight during a race.

Refreshment stations are situated at 5km intervals along the course. In addition to drinks, they also provide sponges, which runners use to cool themselves down.

Bottle which runners carry with them.

Foil wraps

As athletes sweat profusely during a race there is a good chance of them catching a chill when they stop running, as the actual temperature around them may be quite low. To help prevent this, they may use foil wraps to maintain their body temperature.

Hurdling

The three major hurdle events are the 100m (women only), 110m (men only) and 400m. These are essentially sprint races in which athletes also have to clear ten hurdles.* For the spectator, the hurdles make it easier to see who is in the lead, as the leader is simply the athlete who rises first at the hurdle.

The athletes participating in these events are generally taller than those in sprint races. The hurdles are highest (106.7cm) in the men's 110m race, so it is an advantage for athletes in this race to have long legs. For women, however, height is not so important as their hurdles are set much lower. In fact, if they have very long legs they may be forced to adjust their natural stride during the 100m, as the hurdles are very close together.

Technique

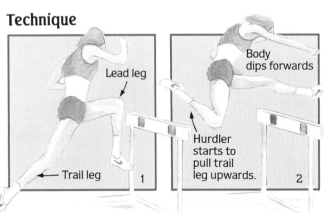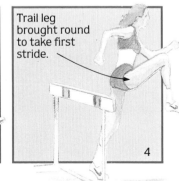

The hurdler's action should appear to be one of continuous sprinting, with only a slight deviation as she skims over each hurdle.

As the athlete approaches the hurdle, she picks up her lead leg with the knee bent (picture 1). She then stretches her leg forward, aiming her heel at the hurdle. She dips her body and throws her opposite arm forward for balance. As her lead leg crosses the hurdle, she starts to pull up her trail leg (picture 2). To prevent her trail knee or foot knocking the hurdle, she pulls her trail leg up and outwards so that her knee is almost under her armpit and her foot is turned outwards (picture 3).

She should pull her lead leg down to the track as quickly as possible, then quickly follow through with her trail leg to recommence her normal sprinting action (picture 4).

The experienced hurdler clears each obstacle quickly and smoothly, losing contact with the ground for as short a time as possible. This is because an athlete loses speed in the air. As any loss of speed will have been multiplied ten times by the end of a race, it is vital that hurdlers perfect their technique.

Stride patterns

A good hurdling rhythm is based on the athlete taking a pre-set number of strides between each hurdle. This is known as the *stride pattern*. In the 100m or 110m race, athletes take three strides between each hurdle, and always lead with the same leg.

In the 400m race, athletes' strides gradually shorten due to fatigue. This forces them to take more strides between hurdles at the end of the race, and they therefore need to be able to lead with either leg. Men usually increase their strides from 13 or 14 to 15, and women from 15 or 16 to 17. This is known as *changing down*.

Athletes must know when they are going to change down, as trying to fit in an extra stride just before the hurdle disrupts their rhythm. Athletes must also work out their stride pattern from the start to the first hurdle (usually 8 strides in the 100/110m and around 20-23 strides in the 400m). This guarantees a good approach to the first hurdle and ensures good rhythm for the rest of the race.

■ The women's 100m hurdles. At this distance, athletes take three strides between each hurdle throughout the race.

Top athletes can run a hurdles race in only one to two seconds more than their times for the equivalent flat race.

Clearing the hurdles

During a race you may notice that even top athletes knock down several of the hurdles while racing. An athlete is not penalized for this, but it will throw him off-balance and slow him down. Athletes are not, however, allowed to trail a leg or foot around the outside of the hurdle (as shown on the right). In the two shorter races this is only possible in the inside and outside lanes as the hurdles touch each other across the track. It is, however, fairly common in the 400m as the hurdles are staggered.

Leg trailing round the outside of the hurdle. Athletes are disqualified for doing this.

Training

A hurdler's training is very similar to that of a sprinter, as he requires similar strength and speed. However, he must also concentrate on improving his hurdling rhythm and his technique for crossing the hurdle. His training will therefore include hopping and jumping exercises, as well as specific hurdling drills.

One such drill is to run by the side of the hurdles clearing them with only the trail leg, in order to improve hip rotation. Hurdlers also carry out mobility exercises to increase their range of movement, especially in the hip area.

An exercise to improve mobility.

The athlete lays his leg along the hurdle then bends forwards. This stretches muscles at the back of his leg.

Top international times

	100m	110m	400m
Men	⎯	under 13.5 secs	under 49.5 secs
Women	under 12.95 secs	⎯	under 55.57 secs

Equipment

The hurdles

Hurdles consist of two adjustable metal stands which support a central wooden bar. Hurdles are not fixed to the track but are held down by weights in the base. For a competition, these weights are set so that a force of at least 3.6kg is required to knock the hurdle over.

During any race each athlete must clear ten hurdles. The height and positioning of these hurdles varies according to the event, as shown in the chart on the right.

	Event	Height of hurdles	Distance from start to first hurdle	Distance between hurdles	Distance from last hurdle to finish
Men	110m	106.7cm	13.72m	9.14m	14.02m
	400m	91.4cm	45m	35m	40m
Women	100m	84cm	13m	8.5m	10.5m
	400m	76.2cm	45m	35m	40m

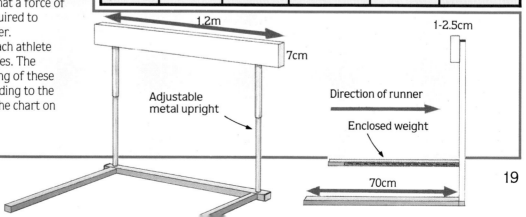

1.2m

7cm

1-2.5cm

Adjustable metal upright

Direction of runner

Enclosed weight

70cm

Steeplechase

This race is considered the most gruelling of all endurance events and is at present run only by men. Athletes run a distance of 3,000m (7.5 laps), and clear four wooden barriers and one water jump on each lap.

Steeplechase runners are likely to have a similar physique to long distance runners. They may, however, be slightly more muscular, as clearing the obstacles requires considerable strength. Many athletes move to this event having achieved success at cross-country or long distance track events.

Athletes should stay in a low, crouched position when stepping on the hurdle.

The athlete's legs should be split as wide as possible, as this helps to keep his body low over the water.

Solid wooden hurdle

The start line

The position of the start line depends on the position of the water jump. Normally this is inside one of the bends but sometimes it is situated outside the track. This affects the length of each lap, so the start line must be adjusted from its normal position on the *back stretch* to ensure that the race is exactly 3,000m.

Clearing the water jump

The most economical way to clear the water jump is for the athlete to step on the hurdle. He places his lead foot on the hurdle with his knee bent and his body leaning slightly forwards. Using his arms for balance, he brings his trail leg up and over the hurdle. As he extends his trail leg ready to land, he pushes off from the hurdle with his lead leg.

It is not a good idea for the athlete to attempt to clear the water, as this would use a lot of energy and interrupt his running action. Instead he lands near the edge of the water so that his next stride carries him on to the track.

Clearing the barriers

A steeplechaser cannot skim over the barriers, as they are made of solid wood and he could injure himself if he were to hit one. He must, however, stay as low over the barriers as possible as any extra height will only waste valuable time.

As he approaches the barrier, the athlete should maintain or even increase his speed. If he slows down, he will be forced to leap rather than hurdle the barrier. This uses more energy and makes it more difficult for the athlete to continue his running action after clearing the barrier.

As the obstacles are placed at irregular intervals around the track, the athlete cannot use a set *stride pattern*. He must therefore, be able to lead with either leg.

cantabrian

■ Although he may step on the barriers, an experienced steeplechaser conserves energy by hurdling them. His technique is similar to that of a 400m hurdler, except that he must pass higher over the barriers.

Tactics

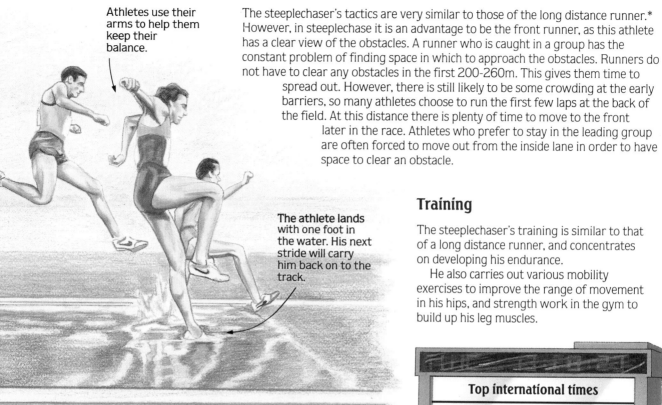

Athletes use their arms to help them keep their balance.

The athlete lands with one foot in the water. His next stride will carry him back on to the track.

On landing, the athlete's lead leg should be taut and the rest of his body well-balanced, ready to resume the running action.

The steeplechaser's tactics are very similar to those of the long distance runner.* However, in steeplechase it is an advantage to be the front runner, as this athlete has a clear view of the obstacles. A runner who is caught in a group has the constant problem of finding space in which to approach the obstacles. Runners do not have to clear any obstacles in the first 200-260m. This gives them time to spread out. However, there is still likely to be some crowding at the early barriers, so many athletes choose to run the first few laps at the back of the field. At this distance there is plenty of time to move to the front later in the race. Athletes who prefer to stay in the leading group are often forced to move out from the inside lane in order to have space to clear an obstacle.

Training

The steeplechaser's training is similar to that of a long distance runner, and concentrates on developing his endurance.

He also carries out various mobility exercises to improve the range of movement in his hips, and strength work in the gym to build up his leg muscles.

Top international times
under 8:21 mins

Equipment

Barriers

Each barrier covers the three inside lanes of the track and overhangs the *infield* by 30cm. Unlike conventional hurdles, these barriers are designed to stand firm when struck. They are made of solid wood and weigh up to 100kg. The upper bar is wide enough for the athlete to stand on if necessary.

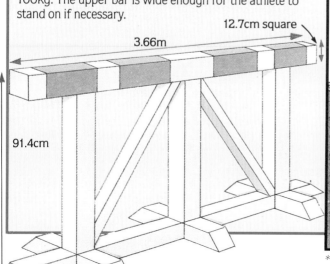

3.66m

12.7cm square

91.4cm

Water jump

The water jump consists of a fixed hurdle, similar to the barriers, in front of which is a 3.66m square expanse of water. The water is deepest in front of the hurdle. From this point the base of the water jump slopes up to track level.

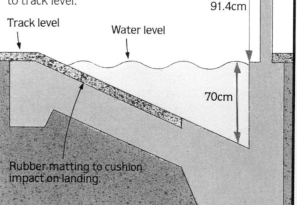

12.7cm

Fixed hurdle

91.4cm

Track level

Water level

70cm

Rubber matting to cushion impact on landing.

* These tactics can be found on pages 14-15.

Cross-country

Cross-country running is an extremely popular sport, attracting as many as 2,000 entrants in one event. The course usually consists of several laps of a 3-5km circuit and involves negotiating natural obstacles such as hills, ploughed land, streams and thick mud. In many countries cross-country courses are now artificially constructed on horse racing tracks or parks. These tend to be flatter and faster than the original cross-country race. As courses can be as long as 12.5km, cross-country is an extremely arduous event.

■ Artificial cross-country courses involve athletes clearing obstacles such as straw bales.

Technique

The cross-country runner's aim is to conserve energy wherever possible. However, because of the varying terrain the runner cannot keep to a steady pace, as on the track. Instead he tries to sustain an even rhythm and to clear any obstacles as economically as possible. On fairly flat ground cross-country runners use the same action as any long distance runner. However, over rough ground athletes adopt a short, quick stride, using their arms for balance.

Where possible, athletes will step on obstacles, such as gates, in a similar fashion to steeplechasers clearing the water jump (see page 20). They will run through any water, as jumping over it would waste energy and affect their rhythm on landing.

When running downhill athletes allow the slope to carry them along, which both lengthens and quickens their stride. Trying to check the natural momentum of running downhill would actually use up more energy.

If running uphill athletes lean forward slightly and shorten their stride.

The finish

The finish area is usually roped off to form one or several narrow channels. Runners enter the channels one at a time and their positions are recorded by race officials at the far end. This is to ensure that each runner is placed in the correct order, as large groups of runners may often finish together.

Training

Although athletes carry out some flat running, the bulk of their training concentrates on dealing with varying terrain. Athletes therefore train on hills, sand and ploughed land, and do large amounts of *fartlek training* (see page 15).

They must also develop their leg muscles through strength and mobility training in the gym.

Equipment

Shoes

These shoes are similar to those used by marathon runners in that they are lightweight and must fit perfectly. They also have a slightly raised heel for added protection. The soles are fitted with a plastic plate, which allows the athlete to fit spikes of varying length to suit the running conditions.

Long spikes for use on grass.

Race walking

Race walking is a modified version of ordinary walking. This modified style is used because it enables athletes to go faster. Normal walking speed is about 8km/h, but top athletes can reach around 15km/h.

Walking events can take place on either road or track and can be any distance from 1500m to 50km. The only recognized international distances, however, are 10km (women), 20km (men) and 50km (men).

The rules

The rules on style and technique are very strict in order to differentiate between walking and running. The most important rule is that an athlete must "make continuous unbroken contact with the ground". This means that his lead foot must touch the ground before he picks up his rear foot. If an athlete breaks this contact, which is known as *lifting*, he will be warned by a judge that he is liable to disqualification. Lifting is most likely to occur at speeds greater than 13-14km/h.

Technique

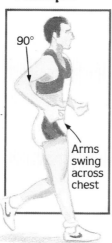
90°
Arms swing across chest

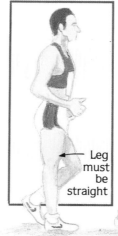
Leg must be straight

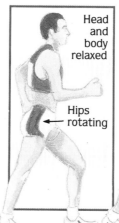
Head and body relaxed
Hips rotating

90°
Both feet on ground

The walker lands on his heel and moves smoothly on to the ball of his foot. His lead leg straightens completely as it takes his full body weight. He does not bring his rear leg forward until his lead leg has made solid contact with the ground. This action is accompanied by an exaggerated hip movement (see below).

The athlete's head and body should appear relaxed and be held upright, while his arms swing across his chest to balance the rotation of the hips. Despite this exaggerated action the walker's overall appearance should be one of smooth continual motion.

Hip movement

The distinctive rolling gait of the walker is caused by the rotation and tilting of his hips.

By rotating his hips as he walks the athlete is able to increase his stride length by around 20cm (see right). The rotation of top walkers is so pronounced that it results in them placing one foot directly in front of the other. In addition to this, the walker tries to keep his body as level as possible by tilting his hips as he walks.

Training

A race walker's training sessions involve strength and stamina exercises such as weight training, hill running and *interval training* (see page 12). The athlete also concentrates on improving his technique; for example, by using hurdling drills to improve his hip mobility.

Ordinary walking

Foot
Level hips
Around 1m

Stride length when hips are not rotated.

Race walking

Around 1.2m
Rotated hips

Increased stride length when hips are rotated.

Top international times

	10km	20km	50km
Men	—	under 1:25 hrs	under 4hrs
Women	under 47mins	—	—

High jump

High jump techniques have always been determined by the landing equipment available. Before the early 1960s only sand pits were used: these did not cushion a jumper's fall and forced athletes to use a technique which guaranteed a safe landing. The development of foam landing areas has encouraged athletes to concentrate exclusively on improving efficiency at take-off and when crossing the bar.

Today, world class jumping is dominated by the *Fosbury flop** technique, which involves the athlete landing on her back. In this event, height is a distinct advantage. Jumpers also need to be light, and to have enough leg strength and spring to propel their bodyweight up to 20-30cm higher than their own height.

■ Stefka Kostadinova breaking the world record in 1987, using the Fosbury flop technique. She keeps her back straight and lifts her hips over the bar.

Technique

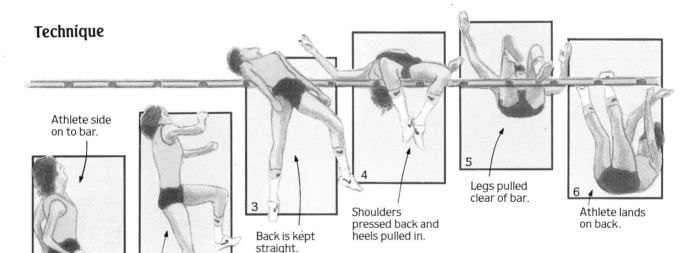

Athlete side on to bar.

Arms swing up.

Back is kept straight.

Shoulders pressed back and heels pulled in.

Legs pulled clear of bar.

Athlete lands on back.

The athlete uses the first half of her approach run to gather speed. There is then a smooth transition into a final, curved approach which places her side-on to the bar. During this final phase (usually around three strides), the athlete leans into the curve and swings her outside arm across her body. Her run changes from a bounding stride to one in which she lands heel first. This enables her to lower her hips so that her take-off leg is flexed (picture 1). At this point she should be travelling at top speed (around 28km/h).

The athlete takes off from the foot furthest away from the crossbar, swinging both arms up to assist her jump (picture 2). On take-off it is her hips that dictate the jumping action. She thrusts them forwards, which in turn pulls her thigh upwards.

The athlete jumps straight up, rather than towards the bar, but due to her curved approach run, her body will naturally turn and propel her head first towards the bar (picture 3). The jumper keeps her back straight and, by pressing her shoulder back and heels in, forces her hips up and away from the crossbar (picture 4).

Once over, the athlete quickly brings her head forwards and knees up to ensure that her feet clear the bar (picture 5). The high jumper lands on her back and shoulders (picture 6).

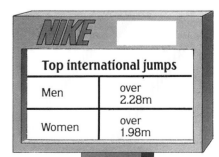

NIKE

Top international jumps	
Men	over 2.28m
Women	over 1.98m

* First used by Dick Fosbury at the 1968 Olympics in Mexico.

Point of take-off

To ensure a safe landing on the foam matting, athletes must take off around 70cm in from the nearer upright.

They must also take off at the right distance from the crossbar so that they reach their highest point directly over the bar. Should they misjudge this distance, they will hit the bar either on their way up or down. This is shown in the diagrams below.

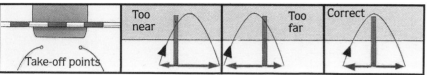

Scoring

Having cleared a qualifying height,* the jumper may enter the competition at any height he chooses, and also choose whether to attempt any subsequent height.

The athlete is allowed to attempt each height three times. However, once he has registered three consecutive failures (not necessarily at the same height) he will be disqualified.

A failure is registered if the athlete:

★ Knocks the bar down.

★ Touches the area beyond the uprights without clearing the bar.

★ Does not attempt his jump within 90 seconds** of taking his position on the runway.

In the event of a tie, the athlete who has made the fewest attempts at the height is the winner. Should the number of attempts be the same, the winner is the athlete with the lowest number of failures throughout the competition.

This scoring system means that an athlete must carefully consider whether or not to attempt each height, as his decision can seriously alter his final position. This is shown in the example below.

Scorecard

	1.73m	1.75m	1.77m	1.80m	1.83m	1.85m	1.88m	Total fail-ures	Total jumps	Final place
A	–	XO	O	XO	–	XXO	All failed at this height	4	8	2=
B	O	O	O	X–	XO	XXO		4	9	2=
C	O	O	X–	O	XXO	XXO		5	10	4
D	O	–	–	XXO	XXO	XO		5	9	1

Key

X = Failed   O = Clear

– = Didn't jump

D is the winner as he has the least number of attempts at 1.85m.

C is fourth as he has more failures than A and B.

A and B have the same number of failures, therefore they share second place.

Training

To improve take-off rhythm and timing when clearing the bar, the high jumper carries out various drills including bounding and mobility (stretching) exercises. These are interspersed with sprint drills to increase speed on approach, and weight training to develop strength. For variety, athletes often practise old high jump techniques such as the straddle.

Equipment

The crossbar and uprights

The high jump consists of a pair of metal uprights, positioned at least 4m apart, which support a fibre glass crossbar. The bar is between 3.98m and 4.02m in length, weighs no more than 2kg, and is striped for easy visibility. It rests on two height-adjustable pegs, but will fall off backwards if struck.

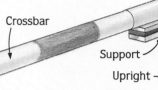

Crossbar

Support

Upright

There is a gap of at least 1cm between the support and the crossbar.

Although there is a measuring system incorporated into the uprights, the height is also checked manually each time the crossbar is raised or when a record is broken.

Shoes

These are similar to the spiked running shoes used by track runners, however the soles and heels may be fitted with up to eleven spikes.

Heel spikes ensure firm contact with ground.

*Qualifying rounds only occur in major championships.
**This time limit applies to all field events except the pole vault where two minutes are allowed.

Long jump

To be a successful long jumper it is vital be a fast sprinter, as the speed of the approach run has a direct effect on the length of a jump. The long jumper's physique is, therefore, very similar to that of the sprinter: tall, long-legged, and strongly built, with good *explosive power*.

As top jumpers are capable of reaching speeds of up to 41km/h on their approach run, it is not suprising that many of them also have exceptionally good 100m times.

Technique

The long jump can be divided into four distinct phases: the approach, the take-off, the flight and the landing.

The approach

The jumper must hit the take-off board at top speed and in perfect balance. An accurately paced run is therefore vital, and the athlete has a set *stride pattern* for his approach run. Most athletes place a *checkmark* about ten strides from the take-off board to ensure that their run-up is correct. If they are not on the right stride when they reach the mark, they will stop and begin again.

The approach run consists of about 19-21 strides. The athlete reaches his ideal speed by the fourteenth or fifteenth stride: if he were to accelerate after this, his take-off would be uncontrolled. During the final strides, he brings his hips forward in preparation for the take-off. This alters his running action, making his strides shorter and his knee pick-up higher.

■ As speed is vital during the approach run, Carl Lewis's exceptional sprinting power is a great advantage in his long jumping.

The take-off

The athlete strikes the take-off board with the whole of his foot, quickly pulling it back behind him.* Thrusting his hips upwards and forwards, he does not try to jump from the board, but runs off it with his body almost upright. This fast action allows him to drive vigorously both upwards and forwards, rather than primarily upwards, which would lead to a loss of distance.

The flight

The athlete can increase the distance he travels by slowing down his body's tendency to tip forwards, which would result in a premature landing. He does this by employing one of two flight styles: the *hitchkick* or the *hang jump*.

The hitchkick: The athlete takes one or two strides in mid-air, before drawing both legs forwards for landing.
▼

The hang jump: Here the jumper appears to hang momentarily in the air before swinging her arms and legs forwards, ready for landing. ▶

The jumper should cover at least 15cm of the board with his take-off foot.

The landing

An athlete's jump is measured* from the take-off board to the nearest mark in the sand, which is usually made by her bottom or heels. She therefore tries to land in such a way that she touches the ground at the last possible moment.

The athlete throws her legs forward as far as possible, and deliberately allows her heels to skid along the surface of the sand. This is called *shooting through*.

By throwing her arms forwards and bending her knees, the athlete prevents her body from falling backwards as she skids. A top athlete can reach the original mark made by her feet before her bottom touches the sand, thus considerably lengthening her jump.

After the jump, the athlete must not walk back through the pit after her attempt, or the jump will be invalid.

1. On landing, the athlete throws her arms forward, and bends her knees.

Original mark

2. She is then able to skid along to the original mark made by her heels.

Training

The long jumper will carry out similar training routines to those of a sprinter, including multiple runs over short distances, accelerations, and even work from the blocks. She will also do a lot of hopping and bounding exercises in order to develop her strength and sense of rhythm. In addition, an athlete may carry out various hurdling routines to improve her judgement of distances and balance.

NIKE
Top international jumps

Men	over 8m
Women	over 6.75m

Equipment

Take-off board

The wooden take-off board is embedded in the runway level with the surface. The edge nearest the pit, or landing area, is known as the take-off line and any athlete stepping beyond this line is deemed to have failed at that attempt.

To detect any error, a raised layer of plasticine is placed on the edge of the board nearest to the pit. Any athlete who steps over the board will leave a clear imprint.**

Plasticine

Rigid block support

Take-off board

30°

10cm

10cm   20cm

Shoes

Long jumpers wear shoes similar to those of sprinters. Sometimes the soles are fitted with an extra spike to improve their grip on the smooth take-off board. Atheles may also use padding or plastic heel cups in their shoes to provide extra cushioning for their heels.

Additional spike

NIKE

1.22m

2m

9m

Take-off board

Take-off line

Pit or landing area

The sand in the landing area is level with the runway surface.

Minimum width 2.75m

* You can read about measuring and scoring systems for this event on page 29.
** A no-jump is indicated by the raising of a red flag.

Triple jump

The triple jump is perhaps the most demanding of all the jumping events as it requires great strength and stamina. At international level, it is currently contested by men only.

The triple jump is a technically complex event, as the athlete must take a hop, step and jump whilst trying to cover the maximum possible distance. Triple jumpers therefore require a diverse range of abilities. These include speed, balance and co-ordination, combined with great leg strength.

The three stages of the triple jump

As there are three distinct phases in this event, triple jumpers, unlike long jumpers, must be able to keep going after the initial take-off and landing. It is therefore vital that jumpers distribute their energy evenly over all three stages and maintain speed wherever possible. The jumper's effort should ideally be distributed as follows: hop – 37%, step – 30%, jump – 33%.

During the first two stages he should stay fairly low, as any extra height will result in a loss of speed and forward motion. Staying low also makes his landings easier, as the higher he jumps, the greater the shock to his legs on landing. A heavy landing breaks his rhythm.

■ During the step phase, Willie Banks (USA) keeps his body as straight and low as possible. so that on landing his rhythm is not adversely affected.

Technique

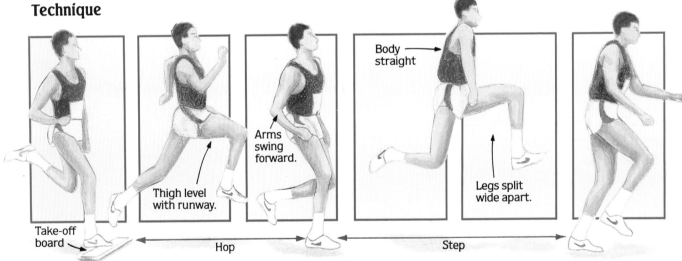

Body straight

Arms swing forward.

Thigh level with runway.

Take-off board

Hop

Legs split wide apart.

Step

During his approach run and final landing the triple jumper's technique is identical to that of the long jumper (see pages 26-27). However between take-off and landing the three distinct techniques of the hop, step and jump are carried out. During each phase the jumper's trail leg must not touch the ground before the final landing.*

Hop

The athlete strikes the take-off board with his foot almost flat. He should avoid the temptation to swing both arms forwards, as this would result in him being pulled upwards rather than forwards. The athlete then swings his take-off leg forwards so that his thigh is parallel to the runway. At the same time he swings his other leg backwards to help maintain his balance. While in the air, his upper body remains vertical and he should keep as low as possible. On landing he swings his arms forwards to assist his next take-off.

Step

The athlete immediately drives off with his landing leg, swinging his arms and his trail leg forwards to help his momentum. He then virtually hangs in the air. Whilst still in flight, he prepares for the landing by drawing back his arms and then firmly planting his trail leg in front of his body. This puts the athlete in a good position to generate enough lift for the final jump phase.

All other rules are the same as in the long jump.

Equipment

The take-off board, landing area and runway are all the same as those used for the long jump (see page 27). However, for the triple jump the take-off board is placed 13m from the landing area rather than 1.22m.

Measuring device

This consists of a mobile telescopic gun sight attached to a support which runs the length of the landing area. An official places a marker where the athlete landed and the gun sight is lined up with the marker. This then calculates the distance from a fixed point on the take-off line and digitally displays the result.*

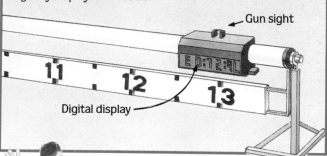

Gun sight

Digital display

Scoring

The scoring system for both the triple jump and the long jump is the same.

The top twelve competitors are allowed three attempts to qualify as one of the eight finalists. These athletes are then given a further three attempts, from which the final placings are decided. Each competitor is placed according to his best jump.

In the event of a tie the next best jumps are compared.

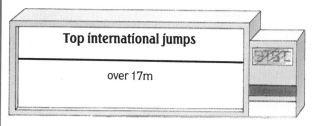

Top international jumps

over 17m

Training

Triple jumpers need greater leg and back strength than long jumpers, as their muscles take an immense pounding on landing during the hop and step phases. In order to withstand this force, jumpers must develop their overall strength and, in particular, the ability of their legs muscles to cope with such a strain.

A lot of their training is devoted to weight training and bounding drills. These drills include multiple hops and bounds on to, over and from boxes and benches; working with weights attached to the legs; the use of sloping surfaces; and variations in speed. Track work similar to that of the sprint hurdler or 200m runner, is also a feature of triple jumpers' training programmes.

Jumper keeps his body as straight as possible using his arms for balance.

Athletes often practise the first and second phase of the triple jump by hopping over hurdles.

The hurdles are set fairly low.

Arms used to keep balance.

Arms and legs thrown forward on final landing.

Athlete uses a simple hang jump.

Jump

Jump

This stage is similar to the long jump as the athlete drives upwards and forwards using a quick striking action. However, by this point the athlete will have lost speed due to his other two landings and uses a *hang jump*, which is the simpler of the two jumping techniques (see page 26). Despite the extra effort involved in the triple jump, top athletes can still clear over 6m in the final jump.

* This measuring device is used for both the long jump and triple jump.

Pole vault

Pole vaulting is probably the most spectacular of all the field events, and is at present restricted to male competitors only.

During this event athletes use a flexible, fibreglass pole to catapult themselves over a bar, which in major events may be higher than 5.5m above the ground. In order to perform the complicated series of movements involved, pole vaulters require a highly developed range of gymnastic skills, great strength and speed.

Gripping and carrying the pole

The vaulter grips the pole firmly with both hands. His top hand* is placed as high up the pole as possible, as this determines the height to which he is eventually carried. He can improve his grip by binding the pole with fabric tape and coating it in lighter fuel or by using resin on his hands. The pole is carried on the opposite side of his body to his take-off foot.

This hand is turned palm upwards to support the pole.

Arm bent

This hand is placed palm down.

The athlete's hands are positioned 60-70cm apart.

The pole is gradually lowered towards the ground during the approach run.

NIKE

Top international jumps
over 5.6m

Technique

In pole vaulting an accurate approach run is vital. Any error in the run-up means that the athlete will be too near or too far from the vaulting box (see right) to plant his pole correctly at take-off.

At the start of his run the athlete holds the pole in an almost vertical position. As he gathers speed he gradually lowers the bottom of the pole, so that two strides before he takes off it is just above the ground. The athlete then plants the bottom of the pole in the back of the vaulting box and pushes the top of the pole upwards.

On take-off the vaulter's take-off foot should be below his top hand

(picture 1). This enables him to push off strongly from the ground. He then hangs from the pole, using his weight to make it bend further (pictures 2-3). This increases the power with which it will straighten to flick him over the bar. He then swings his hips up and round, and tucks his body under the pole (picture 4). This is often referred to as *rocking back*.

He is carried in this position until the pole is almost straight (picture 5). At this point he raises his hips and legs vertically above his hands

(picture 6) and performs a handstand on top of the pole at the moment it finally straightens. This movement enables him to gain a further metre above his grip height. The vaulter lets go of the pole and travels over the crossbar feet first (picture 7). He lands on his back like a high jumper.

Hand and take-off foot in line.

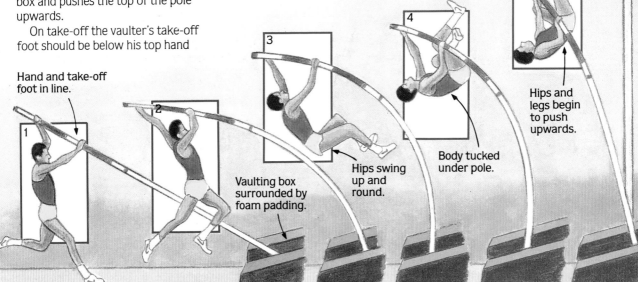

Vaulting box surrounded by foam padding.

Hips swing up and round.

Body tucked under pole.

Hips and legs begin to push upwards.

30   * A right-handed vaulter places his right hand at the top of the pole and a left-hander his left.

Scoring

The system of scoring in pole vault is the same as that in high jump (see page 25), with an athlete being disqualified if he fails on three consecutive vaults. A failure is registered if the athlete does any of the following:

★ Knocks the bar down with his body or with the pole.

★ Repositions his hands once he is airborne.

★ Does not attempt his vault within two minutes of positioning himself on the runway.

★ Touches the area beyond the uprights with his body or the pole before his vault.*

Training

As the pole vaulter needs excellent gymnastic abilities, a lot of his training is devoted to gymnastic and trampolining routines, which help to give him the feel of the various positions in flight.

His strength and stamina are improved through cross-country runs and track work. He does gym work to improve the power of his muscles (especially those in his upper body), as well as specialized work with the pole.

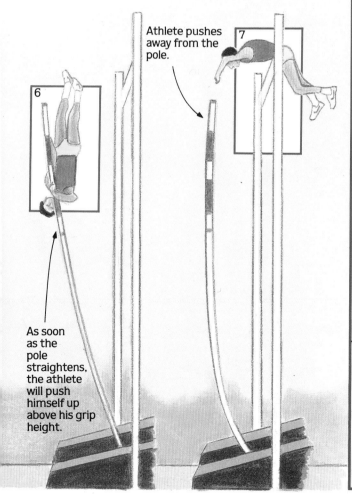

Athlete pushes away from the pole.

As soon as the pole straightens, the athlete will push himself up above his grip height.

Equipment

The crossbar and uprights

The basic structure and arrangement of the crossbar and uprights are the same as in the high jump (see page 25), except that the uprights must now be at least 4.3m apart. Because of the height involved, the bar is placed on the two supports and these are then winched up to the correct height, which is displayed on a gauge in one of the uprights. The height of the bar is increased by about 5-10cm each time.

Support

Gauge

Winch

The vaulting box

This is a sloping metal box, situated beneath the crossbar. It slopes from track level to a depth of 20cm, and narrows from 60cm in width down to 15cm.

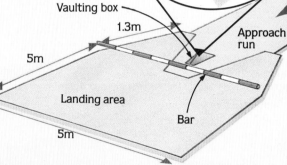

Vaulting box
Track level
1m
15cm
60cm
Approach run

The landing area

Vaulting box
1.3m
5m
Approach run
Landing area
Bar
5m

Since the athlete falls from a considerable height, the landing area must be designed to ensure that he can land safely. If the landing area is too hard the athlete may injure himself, but if it is too soft he may sink through it and hit the ground (known as *bottoming out*). To ensure the athlete's fall is broken gradually, the landing area is made from different densities of foam. There is also additional padding on either side of the vaulting box in case the pole snaps** or fails to straighten, forcing the athlete to land on the wrong side of the bar.

Pole

The pole is made of fibreglass, is around 5m long and weighs 2kg. It must be able to bend to an angle of 90°. The tip of the pole is fitted with a replaceable rubber bung or stopper, to protect it in the vaulting box.

* The pole may fall through the uprights after a vault as long as the bar is not dislodged.
** If the pole snaps it will not count as a failed attempt.

Shot put

The shot put involves throwing a heavy metal ball (the shot) and consequently some of the most powerful athletes are found in this event. Despite their size, however, they must have exceptional speed to put the shot successfully. In fact, most shot putters can run as fast as a sprinter over 30m.

What makes a good throw?

When an athlete throws an object such as the shot or hammer, the distance it travels is determined by the speed, height and angle at which it is released. In order to maximize the distance of the throw, the object must be released as high and as fast as possible, at an angle of around 45° to the ground (see diagram). If the angle of release is lower than this, the object may travel quickly, but it will not remain airborne long enough to gain distance. If the angle is higher, the object will remain airborne longer, but it will travel upwards rather than forwards.

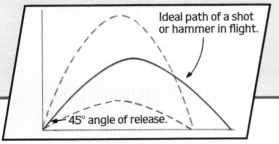

Ideal path of a shot or hammer in flight.

45° angle of release.

Holding the shot

The thrower rests the shot on three fingers of her putting (throwing) hand, supporting it on either side with her thumb and little finger. She may improve her grip by applying chalk or resin to her hands. The shot should not touch the palm of her hand at any time during the putting action. She holds the shot against her chin, with her putting hand resting on her shoulder and the elbow held high.

Technique

Athletes use one of two techniques. The more common style is the *linear* or *O'Brien technique* (named after its creator, Parry O'Brien) which is described below. Gaining in popularity, however, is the *rotational technique* which is similar to the method used in discus (see pages 36-37).

O'Brien technique

The athlete stands at the back of the circle facing away from the landing area. She moves backwards across the circle by raising one leg and kicking it towards the front of the circle, whilst pushing off the heel of her support leg. As her support leg straightens and her raised leg reaches the front of the circle, she takes a quick hop backwards landing with her foot turned outwards. This enables her to pivot on the ball of her foot, and rotate her body towards the front of the circle. This rotating movement starts from her foot and hips, with her putting shoulder and arm following through. At the same time, she straightens her body and pushes the shot up and out.

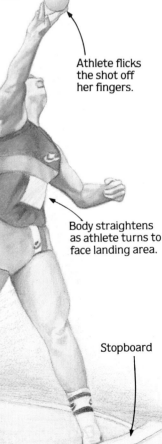

Athlete flicks the shot off her fingers.

The athlete leans forward, bends her knee and raises her other leg behind her.

Body straightens as athlete turns to face landing area.

Body weight on front leg.

Stopboard

Feet positioned one behind the other.

Scoring

The system of scoring in all throwing events is the same, with each athlete being placed according to his best throw. Each of the top twelve competitors is allowed three attempts to qualify as one of the eight finalists. These athletes are then allowed a further three throws each to decide the final placings. In the event of a tie, the athletes' next best throws are compared.

An athlete will register a failure if:

★ The shot lands outside the landing sector.

★ The thrower leaves the circle or touches the ground outside the circle.

★ The thrower touches the top of the stopboard (see below).

■ Ilona Slupianek, using the O'Brien technique, competes in the 1978 European Championships.

Top international throws	
Men	over 20m
Women	over 19m

Training

Although the athlete must develop her arm and shoulder muscles, her training concentrates on strengthening the muscles in her legs and torso, as these take most of the strain. The athlete devotes a lot of time to weight training, bounding and hopping exercises, sprint drills and weight lifting. The athlete also increases her overall bodyweight by keeping to a high protein diet.

Bent knee sit-ups are a good way to strengthen the abdominal muscles.

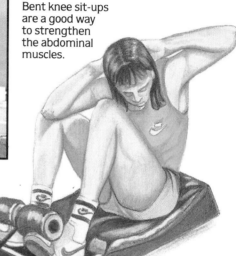

The athlete's feet are placed under weights.

Equipment

Landing area

The shot must land in a 40° sector which is clearly marked on the ground by white lines. To help spectators gauge the length of a throw, the area is divided into a series of arcs 1m apart.

Circle

The shot is thrown from a flat, concrete circle , 2cm below ground level. It measures 2.135m in diameter and is surrounded by a metal rim. The front of the circle is fitted with a wooden stopboard which prevents the athlete stepping out of the circle. Both the stopboard and the circle are painted white.

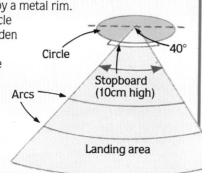

Circle

40°

Stopboard (10cm high)

Arcs

Landing area

Shot

The shot is a smooth, solid, iron or brass ball, which weighs 7.26kg for the male events and 4.00kg for the female events.

Shoes

Shot putters wear shoes which have smooth, slightly curved rubber soles. These enable them to turn easily in the throwing circle.*

Slightly curved sole.

Clothing

A shot putter may wear a large leather belt. This helps to support his back muscles when they are being used to stabilize the spine during the putting action.

Similar shoes are also used by discus and hammer throwers.

Hammer

This is probably the most dramatic and dangerous throwing event, and at international level is only contested by men. The hammer is thrown from the same circle as the shot put, and these powerful athletes must be extremely agile and quick to perform the complex rotational movements within it.

The path of the hammer ▶

The athlete swings the hammer so that as it moves round it also travels up and down, with the high point occurring behind the athlete and the low point in front. This action enables him to release the hammer at the correct angle of 45° (see page 32), as the hammer is already travelling in its intended direction. If the athlete were to swing the hammer round parallel to the ground he would find this much harder, as he would have to alter the direction in which the hammer was already moving (see diagrams).

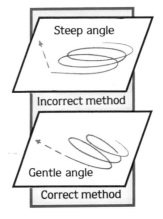

Steep angle

Incorrect method

Gentle angle

Correct method

■ The athlete requires exceptional balance in order to pivot on just the outside of his foot.

◀ The grip

The athlete holds the hammer by firmly gripping the handle in his leading hand. It is vital that he wears a protective leather glove on this hand, as the friction caused by the hammer on its release can rip the skin from his fingers. The athlete then places his other hand over the top of his lead hand.

Technique

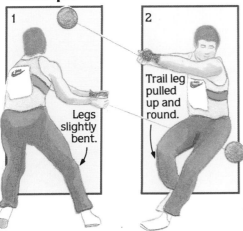

1

2 Trail leg pulled up and round.

Legs slightly bent.

3 Outstretched arms

4 Athlete turns on toe and heel.

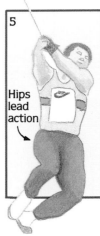

5 Hips lead action

The athlete stands at the back of the circle, facing away from the landing sector. His feet are shoulder-width apart and his knees slightly bent. Whilst still stationary, he swings the hammer round to allow it to gather speed (known as *winding up*) and to give himself time to adjust his balance. On the second turn, as the hammer begins to rise (picture 1), the athlete swivels round on the heel of his lead foot and toe of his trail foot (picture 2). As he turns he quickly pulls his trail leg up and down close to his other knee, so that he pivots on the ball of his small toe. When his trail foot touches the ground his feet are in the same position as at the start (picture 3), ready to repeat the movement (pictures 4-7). This means that his feet and hips have not only caught up with the hammer but are now ahead of it.

This is not a smooth rotational movement: the athlete's hips and body lead the hammer at its high point, then there is a slight pause as

Training

Hammer throwers require immense strength, as by the time the hammer reaches its final turn its head will seem to weigh many times its actual weight. Their training concentrates on developing their strength, especially in the leg and back muscles. They do this mainly through weight training.

As in all throwing events, *explosive power* is very important, so bounding and sprinting exercises form an important part of all hammer throwers' training routines. In order to improve their technique and overall flexibility they also carry out work in the gym, including mobility exercises, *circuit training* and gymnastics.

Top international throws
over 80m

Rules

The same scoring system is used for the hammer as for the shot put (see page 33), and the circle and landing sector used are also the same.

The athlete will register a failure if:

★ He touches the ground outside the circle.

★ The hammer lands outside the landing sector.

However, he will be allowed to throw again if:

★ He loses his rhythm, as long as the hammer has not touched the ground outside the circle.

★ The wire snaps during the throw or in the air.

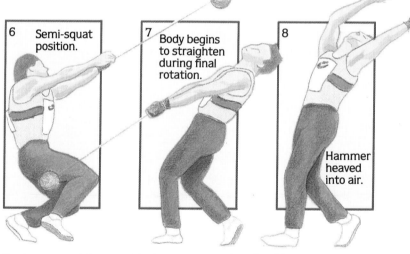

6 Semi-squat position.

7 Body begins to straighten during final rotation.

8 Hammer heaved into air.

the hammer catches up at its low point. The athlete is trying to accelerate the hammer's movements and must keep ahead of it and pull it round.

As he spins the athlete adopts a semi-squat position in order to counteract the weight of the hammer. He holds the hammer at arm's length,

as bending his arms would reduce the speed at which the hammer head is travelling. The athlete rotates two or three times, then on the final turn he heaves the hammer up over his lead shoulder (picture 8). Straightening his legs and body during this movement helps to increase the power behind the throw.

The hammer

The hammer consists of a solid metal ball which is connected to a metal handle by a length of steel wire. The total weight of the hammer is 7.260kg.

The overall length of the hammer, when measured from the inside of the grip, is 121.5cm.

Iron ball

Hammer cage

It is quite easy for even top athletes to release the hammer in the wrong direction. The rear of the throwing area is therefore surrounded by a cage to protect officials and spectators. The hammer cage consists of several steel uprights which support heavy netting.

Measuring device

All throwing events are measured in the same way. An official places a marker at the point where the object landed. Then a separate measuring device, using a laser, calculates the distance from the marker to a fixed point at the edge of the throwing area.

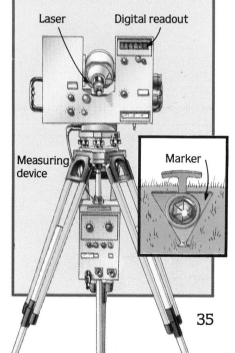

Laser

Digital readout

Measuring device

Marker

Discus

This event involves athletes rotating across the throwing circle and releasing a flat circular object, known as a discus. The rules governing the discus are the same as those for the shot and hammer (see page 35), and the event is open to both men and women.

Although discus throwers must have the same strength as other throwers, they tend to be taller with longer limbs. They also need perfect balance and co-ordination as this technique is far quicker than those used in either the shot or hammer.

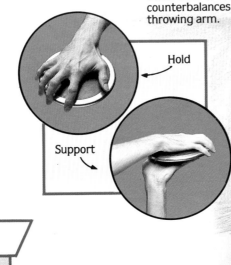

Athlete preparing to commence her rotation.

Throwing arm is fully extended.

Other arm counterbalances throwing arm.

Hold

Support

Athlete stands with her legs apart.

The hold

The discus rests in the athlete's fingers so that it lies across the palm of her hand. To keep it steady, she presses down on the upper surface with her thumb, and rests the edge on the inside of her wrist. Many athletes apply a substance called venice turpentine to their fingers in order to improve their grip. At the start of her throw the athlete may support the discus on her non-throwing hand.

Equipment

Discus

The discus is made of wood and has a circular metal rim. It has a flat metal plate fixed in the centre of each side, and tapers from the plates to the rim. Both sides of the discus must be identical and completely smooth.

Discus	Men	Women
Weight	2kg	1kg
Diameter	22cm	18cm

The discus is thrown into a 40° landing sector from a circle of 2.5m in diameter. The circle is surrounded by a protective cage.

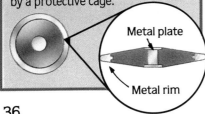

Metal plate

Metal rim

1 Knees bent

2 Weight on pivot leg.

3 Shoulders trail hips.

The athlete positions himself at the back of the circle with his back to the landing sector. He stands with his legs apart, his knees slightly bent and his toes turned outwards (picture 1). He usually carries out one or two preliminary swings before he starts to rotate, in order to gather momentum.

He then shifts his bodyweight on to the leg opposite his throwing arm and, bending his knee, turns on the ball of this foot (picture 2). He rotates by thrusting his hips forward and round, so that his body is twisted away from his other leg and his shoulders are left behind (picture 3). This causes a pull on his trail leg

What makes a good throw?

The discus and the women's javelin* do not fly in the same pattern as the shot and hammer because they have *aerodynamic* qualities. This means that if a discus is at the correct angle by the time it reaches the peak of the arc, the air flowing around it will support it slightly. This enables it to remain in the air longer, and to fly further. To achieve this , the discus must be released at an angle of around 35° to the ground, and also be tilted forward slightly in flight (see diagrams on the right).

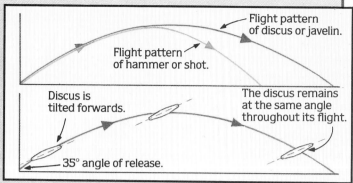

Flight pattern of discus or javelin.

Flight pattern of hammer or shot.

Discus is tilted forwards.

The discus remains at the same angle throughout its flight.

35° angle of release.

◄ **Wind**

Since the discus and the women's javelin are supported by the surrounding air current, their flight pattern is affected by the wind. The most favourable wind is one that approaches the athlete from the directions shown in the diagram on the left. By meeting the discus at this angle, the wind will force the discus upwards, enabling it to travel further.

Favourable wind for a left-handed thrower.

Landing area

Favourable wind for a right-handed thrower.

Top international throws	
Men	over 65m
Women	over 62.5m

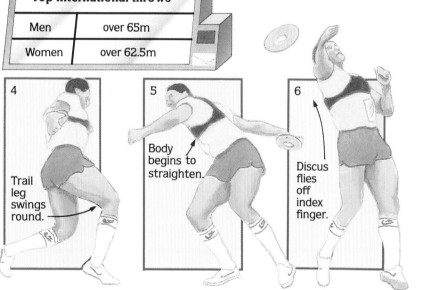

4 Trail leg swings round.

5 Body begins to straighten.

6 Discus flies off index finger.

■ In order to be able to rotate correctly the athlete must concentrate on perfecting his balance.

which swings quickly round to land near the centre of the circle (picture 4). He then continues to pivot on the ball of one foot while bringing his rear foot forward.

As he turns to the front of the circle for the second time, the athlete's hips lead his shoulders (picture 5), so that as he straightens his body, his throwing arm is flung forwards in a wide, swinging motion. This ensures that the discus gathers as much speed as possible. The athlete presses the discus's leading edge down with his thumb so that it is released at the correct angle. The discus then flies off his index finger (picture 6).

Training

A discus thrower's training is similar to that of a shot putter, and includes extensive weight training routines. However, he also devotes a lot of his training time to increasing his speed and mobility.

* See page 38 for why the women's and men's javelins are different.

Javelín

The javelin is the only throwing event in which a throwing circle is not used, as the javelin is thrown while the athlete is on the run. Athletes throw the javelin from a runway into a narrow 29° landing sector.

The physique of most javelin throwers is different from that of other throwers as their main priorities are speed and mobility. Javelin throwers are therefore generally smaller and lighter. However, they still require immense muscle strength in order to throw the javelin successfully, as can be seen by the photograph of Fatima Whitbread on the right.

■ When releasing the javelin, the athlete uses the muscles in her upper body, especially the arms and shoulders.

The design of the javelin

Until 1984 the javelins used in both male and female events were *aerodynamic* (see page 37). However, male athletes were becoming so successful at throwing this type of javelin that there was a danger of it flying beyond the *infield* and on to the track.

The men's javelin was therefore re-designed so that it would not fly so far. This new javelin is no longer aerodynamic and flies in the same manner as the shot or hammer (see page 32).

Holding and carrying the javelin

The athlete holds the javelin by its cord grip, using her hand to provide a stable support in one of the three ways shown on the right.

During the approach run she carries the javelin horizontally above her shoulder. From here, it can be easily moved into the correct throwing position.

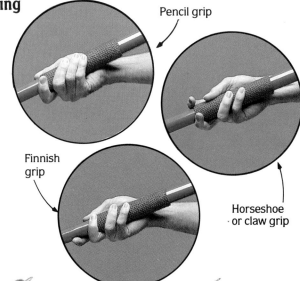

Pencil grip

Finnish grip

Horseshoe or claw grip

Technique

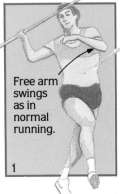

Free arm swings as in normal running.

1

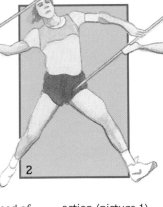

2

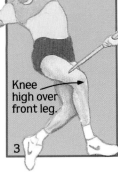

Knee high over front leg.

3

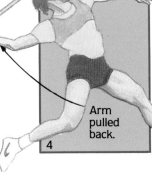

Arm pulled back.

4

The athlete must judge the speed of her run-up carefully. She needs to run as quickly as possible, but still maintain control when releasing the javelin. She lifts her knees high as she runs and swings her free arm as in a normal running

action (picture 1).

During her last few strides the thrower stretches her throwing arm back behind her body, so that she is holding the javelin at arm's length (picture 2). This position enables her to use the additional power in

her trunk muscles when she releases the javelin. However, it also causes the athlete's shoulder and hips to be dragged round to the side, which in turn slows her down. The athlete therefore lifts her knee on her throwing side high over her front

Rules

Perhaps the most important rule is that the javelin must land point first for a throw to be valid. However, this does not mean that it must stick in the ground. A javelin will often land point first and then bounce further on along the ground. If this should happen then the throw will be measured from the first mark made by the javelin.

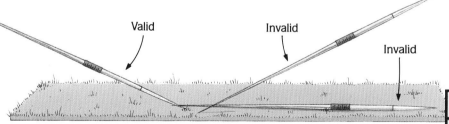

Valid

Invalid

Invalid

A throw will only be valid if:

★ The javelin is thrown overarm.

★ The javelin lands within the landing sector.

★ The athlete remains behind the scratch line until the throw has been measured.

★ The athlete faces the landing area at all times.

Top international throws	
Men	over 80m
Women	over 67.5m

Training

The requirements of this event are speed, mobility and elastic strength. The athlete's training therefore stresses such activities as bounding, ball throwing, mobility exercises and speed training, all of which help to increase his muscle speed and reactions.

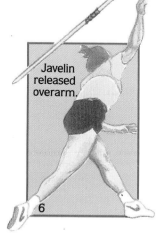

Back arched

5

Javelin released overarm.

6

leg, and lands with her foot pointing straight ahead (picture 3). This forces her hips to turn forwards, and is often referred to as the *cross-over step*.

The athlete then moves her hips forward ahead of her shoulders (picture 4), so that her body appears to arch backwards (picture 5). This enables her shoulder to be catapulted forwards, bringing the throwing arm through to release the javelin high over her shoulder (picture 6).

Equipment

Javelin

The javelin is a metal or wooden shaft with a sharp, pointed metal head. There is a cord hand grip positioned near the middle. The javelin gradually tapers from this grip towards each end.

The dimensions of the javelin vary according to the competitor's sex, as shown below.

Javelin	Men	Women
Length	2.6-2.7m	2.2-2.3m
Weight	800g	600g
Length of grip	15-16cm	14-15cm
Maximum diameter	25-30cm	20-25cm

Runway and landing area

The runway is 4m wide and between 30m and 36.5m long. A curved *scratch line* is marked at the throwing end.

The javelin must be thrown into a 29° landing sector. This is divided up into a series of arcs 10m apart which make it easier to judge the length of a throw.

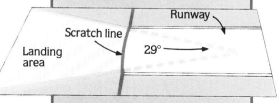

Runway

Scratch line

Landing area

29°

Shoes

As javelin throwers take a lot of strain on their ankles during the run-up, they wear high-sided boots which provide additional support. These boots have spikes in both the heel and the sole in order to improve the grip on the runway.

High sides to support ankles.

The decathlon and heptathlon

The decathlon, in which only men compete, consists of ten events and the heptathlon, which is for women, consists of seven. They are both two-day contests, and are held to find the best all-round male and female athletes. Multi-event athletes are relatively tall and must have a well-balanced physique. These competitions consist mainly of sprinting and field events, and therefore favour athletes with great explosive power. However, as their training requires several hours of work each day, they must also have a certain level of endurance.

It is unlikely that a multi-event athlete could match the performance of specialist athletes in every single event. It is not unusual though for them to excel in at least one of the events. Many, in fact, begin their athletic careers as specialists in an individual event.

■ Decathlon

The modern decathlon was first held in 1911 in Germany, when all ten events took place on the same day. It was introduced to the Olympics in 1912 when, as today, it was held over two days. Most athletes score more points on the first day, as the two most difficult events, the pole vault and the 1500m, are both held on the second day. They may also be fatigued and stiff from the previous day.

■ Day two
3. pole vault

■ Day one
5. 400m

■ Day one
4. high jump

■ Day two
2. discus

■ Day one
2. long jump

■ Day one
1. 100m

■ Day one
3. shot put

■ Day two
1. 110m hurdles

Organizing the events

The multi-event competitions attract large numbers of entrants and preliminary rounds, within the two day period, are often required. In track events, athletes run in *heats*. These are drawn so that the leading point scorers run together. This ensures that they compete under the same conditions (for example, wind speed). In throwing events athletes are randomly divided into two groups which compete simultaneously, or one after the other. The jumping events are organized so that athletes with the best performances compete in the same group.

As athletes will have to wait to compete, they prevent their muscles tightening (which can lead to injury) by keeping warm in blankets or sleeping bags.*

Training

Multi-event athletes need a wide range of athletic skills. These include speed, strength, suppleness and agility. To acquire these qualities, multi-event athletes train harder and longer than any others. Their training must be carefully balanced so that they do not concentrate on one event to the detriment of another.

Rules

The rules are the same as those for individual events, except that in track events athletes are allowed an extra *false start* and in throwing events and the long jump athletes are permitted just three attempts.

Athletes must start each event otherwise they are disqualified. If they fail to complete an event, however, they simply score no points in that event.

Top international scores	
Men	over 8,000 points
Women	over 6,000 points

■ Heptathlon

The heptathlon was introduced in 1981 to replace the pentathlon (five events) which favoured faster, lighter women. By introducing the javelin and the 800m there is now greater emphasis on strength.

Many athletes find the shot put difficult, as they do not have a heavy physique and increasing their body weight might ruin their other events.

*Some stadiums also set aside a rest room.

Scoring

The winner is determined by a total number of points accumulated throughout the competition. An athlete scores points according to the time, distance or height achieved in each event. The better the performance, the more points awarded. Each possible result, along with the corresponding score, is listed in a book, which officials then consult.

It is possible for an athlete to win the competition without having won an individual event. If there is a tie, the winner is the athlete who has been placed highest in the majority of events, and failing that, the athlete with the highest score in a single event.

To achieve a top international score, an athlete should average 850 points per event in the heptathlon, or 800 points in the decathlon. Below you can see approximately how many points an athlete would score for the heights, times and distances listed.

■ Decathlon

Points	100m	Long jump	Shot put	High jump	400m	110m hurdles	Discus	Pole vault	Javelin	1500m
1000	10.39 secs	7.76m	18.4m	2.21m	46.17 secs	13.8 secs	56.18m	5.29m	77.2m	3:53.79 mins
900	10.82 secs	7.36m	16.79m	2.11m	48.19 secs	14.59 secs	51.4m	4.97m	70.68m	4:07.42 mins
800	11.27 secs	6.95m	15.16m	2m	50.32 secs	15.41 secs	46.6m	4.64m	64.1m	4:21.77 mins
700	11.75 secs	6.51m	13.53m	1.89m	52.58 secs	16.29 secs	41.72m	4.3m	57.46m	4:36.96 mins
600	12.26 secs	6.06m	11.89m	1.77m	54.98 secs	17.23 secs	36.8m	3.94m	50.74m	4:53.2 mins

■ Heptathlon

Points	100m hurdles	High jump	Shot put	200m	Long jump	Javelin	800m
1000	13.85 secs	1.82m	17.07m	23.8 secs	6.48m	57.18m	2:07.63 mins
900	14.56 secs	1.74m	15.58m	24.86 secs	6.17m	52.04m	2:14.52 mins
800	15.32 secs	1.66m	14.09m	25.97 secs	5.84m	46.88m	2:21.77 mins
700	16.12 secs	1.57m	12.58m	27.14 secs	5.5m	41.68m	2:29.47 mins
600	16.97 secs	1.48m	11.07m	28.4 secs	5.15m	36.46m	2:37.7 mins

■ Day two
4. javelin

■ Day two
5. 1500m.

■ Day one
4. 200m

■ Day two
3. 800m

■ Day one
2. high jump

■ Day one
3. shot put

■ Day two
1. long jump

■ Day two
2. javelin

■ Day one
1. 100m hurdles

The competition

Major competitions require an enormous amount of preparation. Below you can read about how they are organized: there is information on preliminary rounds, the facilities available to competitors and the procedure during such ceremonies as the medal presentation. There is also a listing of some of the more important milestones in the history of athletics.

Identifying the competitors

Large numbers of athletes may be competing during an event. It is therefore essential that competitors are clearly marked so that officials (and spectators) can accurately identify them.

For team events, all athletes are required to compete in their team's colours. In addition to this, each athlete is also required to wear a number which is allocated to him before the competition. This number must be worn on both the front and back of the athlete's vest. In races where photo finish equipment is used, runners must also wear their numbers on the side of their shorts so that they can be easily identified on the film.

Preliminary rounds

The number of competitors entering a major event is usually far greater than the number who can take part in the final. Preliminary rounds are therefore held in order to eliminate a large number of the competitors.

In running events, *heats* are held for all races except the marathon and walking events. Athletes qualify for subsequent rounds on their finishing positions (for example, the first four in each heat go through). In addition, a number of the fastest losers may also qualify. It may take a number of rounds of heats until the athletes are whittled down to around eight to twelve finalists, depending on the event.

Athletes must jump or throw a specified height or distance in order to reach the finals of a field event. If too few achieve this target, those closest also qualify so that there are twelve finalists. If too many qualify, all compete in the final.

Athletes performances during these preliminary rounds (including any records they may set) have no bearing on the result of the final.

Training

During any competition, it is vital that athletes have adequate facilities for training and warming up. Many stadiums, therefore, have additional track and field facilities situated close by, which are at the athletes' disposal throughout the competition.

In order to perform well and without fear of injury, a top athlete must warm-up for at least an hour before competing.

For running events this involves steady jogging in order to warm the muscles, followed by faster runs to stretch and loosen them.

For hurdling and field events, athletes concentrate on stretching and mobility exercises in order to keep their legs, hips, arms and shoulder muscles supple.

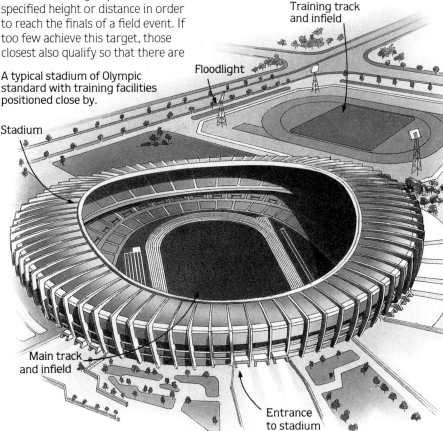

A typical stadium of Olympic standard with training facilities positioned close by.

Training track and infield

Floodlight

Stadium

Main track and infield

Entrance to stadium

Accommodation

At any major championship athletes are provided with accommodation as near to the main stadium and training facilites as possible. In the case of the Olympic Games a large complex, known as the Olympic village, is built nearby. Athletes then live in the village for the duration of the competition.

The opening and closing ceremonies

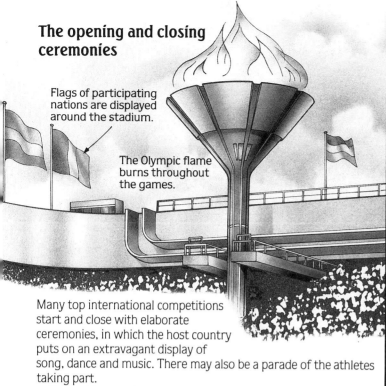

Flags of participating nations are displayed around the stadium.

The Olympic flame burns throughout the games.

Many top international competitions start and close with elaborate ceremonies, in which the host country puts on an extravagant display of song, dance and music. There may also be a parade of the athletes taking part.

During the opening ceremony of the Olympic Games a representative of the host country must swear the Olympic oath, in which, on behalf of all competitors, he promises to abide by the rules and take part in the true spirit of sportsmanship. The Olympic flame is then carried into the stadium having been brought, already lit, from Olympia in Greece by a relay of runners. The flame was first introduced at the 1928 games in Amsterdam, and symbolizes the endeavour for perfection and the struggle for victory.

The medal ceremony

During a major competition the completion of each event is usually followed by a medal ceremony. This usually takes place on the *infield,* close to the *home stretch.*

An Olympic medal

The inscription and detail are the same for gold, silver and bronze in all events.

During the ceremony, gold, silver and bronze medals are presented to the first, second and third athletes respectively. In the Olympics these medals will normally be made of: gold-plated silver, solid silver and solid bronze.

The ceremony is usually finalized by the playing of the victor's national anthem and the raising of the three competitors' national flags.

Athletic milestones

Running

★ First man to run 100m in less than 10 seconds: Jim Hines (USA) at the 1968 Olympics in Mexico City.

★ First woman to run 100m in less than 11 seconds: Renate Stecher (GDR) in 1973.

★ First athlete to run a mile in under four minutes: Roger Bannister (GB) at Oxford in 1954.

★ First athlete to run 10,000m in under 30 minutes: Taisto Maki (Fin) in 1939.

★ First hurdler to complete 110m in under 13 seconds: Renaldo Nehemiah (USA) in 1979.

★ First hurdler to complete 400m in under 50 seconds: Glenn Davis (USA) in 1956. It was only his ninth 400m race.

Throwing

★ First athlete to throw the shot over 21.5m (70ft): Randy Matson (USA) in 1965.

★ First athlete to throw a discus over 70m: Jay Silvester (USA) in 1971.

★ First athlete to throw a hammer over 80m: Boris Zaichuk in 1978.

★ First athlete to throw the javelin over 90m: Terje Pedersen (Nor) in 1980.

Jumping

★ First athlete to clear over 2m in the high jump: George Horine (USA) in 1912.

★ First athlete to pole vault over 5.8m (19ft): Thierry Vigneron (Fra) in 1981.

★ First athlete to clear over 8.9m (29ft) in the long jump: Bob Beamon (USA) at the 1968 Olympics in Mexico City.

★ First athlete to clear 17m in the triple jump: Jozef Schmidt (Pol) in 1960.

Other

★ Only athlete to equal or better six world records within an hour: Jesse Owens (USA) in 1935. They were the 100yds, long jump, 220yds, 200m, 220yds hurdles and 200m hurdles.

★ First athlete to win ten Olympic gold medals: Ray Ewry (USA) between 1900 and 1908. *

★ Largest number of world records to be held by an athlete in one event: high jumper Iolanda Balas (Rom) who has held 14.

---

* This record includes the unofficial games of 1906.

Major athletic competitions

By referring to the chart below, you can find out more about the major athletics competitions held throughout the world. The competitors have usually been selected by their home country.

Competition	When was it first held?	How often it is held?	How long does it run?
AAA/WAA Championships*	Men – 1880 Women – 1922	Every year	2 days
African Games	1985	Every 4 years	12 days
Commonwealth Games (friendly games)	Men – 1930 Women – 1934	Every 4 years	8 days
European Championships	Men – 1934 Women – 1938	Every 4 years	6 days
European Cup	1965	Every 2 years	2 days
European Indoor Championships	1966	Every year**	2 days
Olympic Games	1896	Every 4 years	10 days
Pan-American Games	1937	Every 4 years	9 days
Pan-Arab Games	Men – 1953 Women – 1981	Every 2 years	5 days
World Championships	1983	Every 4 years	9 days
World Cup	1977	Every 4 years	3 days
European Junior Championships	1964	Every 2 years	4 days
World Junior Championships	1986	Every 2 years	5 days
World Student Games (the Universiade)	1924	Every 2 years	7 days

International meets: These are when two or more countries compete in a variety of events, over a period of one to three days. The earliest recorded meet was in 1876 between England and Ireland.

Grand Prix meets: The Grand Prix consists of a number of meets held throughout the year. Invited competitors compete in order to score points towards the final Grand Prix placings. Held annually, each event has an individual winner. There is also an overall Grand Prix winner for both men and women. These meets include – Bislett in Oslo, Peugot-Talbot in London and Weltklasse in Zurich.

Amateur Athletic Association / Women's Amateur Athletic Association
   From 1990 this championship will be held every two years.

Where is it held?	Who can enter?
Different venues throughout England.	Mainly British athletes, though other countries may enter.
Different venues throughout Africa.	Any African nation.
Different venues throughout the Commonwealth.	Any Commonwealth country may enter three athletes in each event.
Different venues throughout Europe.	Athletes who are eligible to represent a European country. There is a limit of three per event.
Different venues throughout Europe.	Each European national team enter one athlete per event.
Different venues throughout Europe.	All European athletes. There is a limit of three athletes per event.
Different venues throughout the world.	Athletes must be amateurs and come from IAAF* member countries.
Different venues throughout the American continent.	Athletes from North and South America.
Different venues throughout the Arab world.	Athletes from the Arab world.
Different venues throughout the world.	Up to three athletes per event from any IAAF member countries.
Different venues throughout the world.	Eight teams are picked to represent the top nations and continents.
Different venues throughout Europe.	European athletes who are under 20 during that year. There is a limit of two athletes per event.
Different venues throughout the world.	Athletes under 20 from any IAAF member country.
Different venues throughout the world.	Competitors must have been involved in full-time education.

IAAF Permit meets: These are the top international meets after the Grand Prix, in which athletes are invited to attend. The organizers will choose which events are included.

EAA Permit meets: These are the top European invitation meets in which athletes compete in a set programme of events. These are chosen by the organizers of the meet.

The will to win

Nowadays many top athletes employ a psychological training coach as well as a physical training coach. This is because an athlete's mental attitude is equally important in determining whether he will win or lose.

Despite years of physical training, all an athlete's hard work can be undone in seconds if he is not properly mentally prepared. To achieve success an athlete is taught that he must:

▨ 1. Want to win (motivation).

▨ 2. Believe he can win (self-confidence).

▨ 3. Keep trying until he wins (persistance).

Motivation

★ An athlete must never be content with second place.

★ His objective is not just to compete, but to win.

Self-confidence

★ An athlete must not allow himself to be intimidated by the occasion or by his opponents.

★ Once in the competition, he must realize that the result is entirely dependent on himself, not on luck or any external factors.

★ He must believe in himself totally.

Persistance

★ The athlete must be able to persist, even when he loses.

★ He must find the motivation to continue training and maintain a positive attitude despite any setbacks.

★ Persistance and determination are probably the most important factors in winning.

* *International Amateur Athletic Federation.*

Glossary

Aerobic system: The system by which an athlete's body produces energy using oxygen.

Aerodynamic: This term is used to describe an object (such as a discus or javelin) which can use the surrounding air currents to help support it in flight.

Alternating runs: A training technique in which an athlete alternates between running at a fast pace and then at a slow pace, over set distances.

Anaerobic system: A system by which an athlete's body uses a fuel stored in the muscles to provide energy without using oxygen.

Back stretch: This is the straight section of the track furthest from the finish.

Bottoming out: This happens when a pole vaulter sinks through a soft landing area and hits the ground.

Boxed in: This happens when an athlete is trapped in the inside lane by athletes immediately in front and to the side of him.

Break: A term for tiring or applying mental pressure to an opponent.

Changing down: During a 400m hurdle race an athlete may need to alter his stride pattern, due to fatigue reducing the length of his stride. He will therefore increase the number of strides he takes between each hurdle.

Change-over: The passing of a baton from one runner to another during a relay race. This must take place within a specific zone.

Checkmarks: These are indicators (such as coloured tape) which an athlete places on the track or runway to ensure a safe change-over in the 4x100m relay, and a correct approach run in jumping events and javelin.

Circuit training: This is a training method in which the athlete performs a series of exercises, repeating each one a set number of times. This is known as a circuit. The athlete then rests and repeats the circuit. He does this a number of times.

Cross-over step: An exaggerated high step used by javelin throwers to ensure that their hips remain facing forwards during the final stages of their approach run.

Dip finish: A lunging dive at the finish line, which a runner uses to beat opponents.

Downsweep pass: A pass used in relay races, in which the incoming runner places the baton down into the receiver's upturned palm.

Elements: These are a type of spike used on running shoes. They are blunter than ordinary spikes and do not puncture the surface of the track. However they still provide the runner with additional grip.

Explosive power: A combination of strength and speed. It is especially important for sprinters and field athletes.

False start: This is committed when an athlete begins to move from the blocks before the starter's gun has been fired.

Fartlek training: A form of training used mainly by middle distance and long distance runners. It involves a continuous run in which athletes alternate their speed according to the terrain. Fartlek is a Swedish term which means 'speed play'.

Flying start: This happens when an athlete is already running as he enters a specific part of a race, such as his leg in a relay.

Fosbury Flop: A high jump technique which involves the athlete travelling head first over the bar on his back.

Hang jump: A technique used by long jumpers in which the athlete hangs in the air before bringing his feet forward to land.

Heat: A preliminary round for track events to decide which athletes will take part in the final.

Hitchkick: A technique used by long jumpers in which the athlete takes one or two steps in the air before bringing both his feet forward to land.

Hitting the wall: The point in a marathon race when a runner experiences a sudden and dramatic increase in fatigue. This is because the athlete's body has exhausted its main supply of energy and has switched to using fat to provide energy.

Home stretch: This is the straight section of the track nearest the main stand, on which the finish line is situated.

Infield: The area situated inside the running track, on which the majority of field events take place.

Interval training: This takes place on a track and involves the athlete alternating between fast and slow runs.

Lapping: This occurs in long distance track races, when runners who have fallen behind are passed by the leaders who are one lap ahead.

Leg: One of the four sections in a relay race.

Lifting: This is an offence in walking events. It occurs when an athlete breaks continual foot contact with the ground.

Linear technique: A technique used by shot putters in which they move backwards across the circle in order to build up speed before putting the shot.

Non-visual change-over: A change-over used in a 4x100m relay, in which the receiver does not look back at the incoming runner when the baton is passed.

O'Brien technique: This is another name for the linear technique in shot putting (see opposite).

Pacemaker: A runner who has been specifically placed in a middle or long distance race in order to set the pace and produce a fast time.

Qualifying round: A preliminary round in which field athletes must clear a pre-determined height or distance in order to ensure a place in the final.

Resistance training: A form of training in which the athlete runs with a weight or in difficult conditions (such as running up hills or in sand) in order to increase his workload.

Rocking back: A technique used by pole vaulters in which the athlete tucks himself up under the pole by swinging his knees up to his chest. He remains in this position until the pole is almost straight.

Rotational technique: A technique used by shot putters, hammer and discus throwers, in which they quickly rotate across the circle before throwing.

Running blind: This happens when an athlete, placed in the outside lane during a staggered start, is unable to see the inside runners who have started behind him.

Scratch line: This is another term for the starting line in any running event, and the throwing line in the javelin.

Shooting through: A technique used by long jumpers to extend the length of their jump, in which they throw their legs forward and allow their heels to skid along the surface of the landing area.

Staggered start: If a race starts on a bend, the athletes' starting positions are staggered, to ensure that they each run the same distance.

Straight start: This is a start in which the runners line up side-by-side across the track.

Stride pattern: A calculated number of strides that a hurdler must take between hurdles in order to be able to take off correctly at each hurdle.

Surging: A tactic used in long distance races, in which the leader will alternately increase and decrease the race pace in order to tire his opponents and disrupt their running rhythm.

Upsweep pass: A pass used in relay races, in which the incoming runner brings the baton up into the palm of the receiver's hand.

Visual change-over: A change-over used in a 4x400m relay, in which the the outgoing runner will turn to watch the incoming runner as the baton is passed.

Warming up: This is a series of exercises which an athlete carries out before a competition in order to prepare himself both physically and mentally. If he does not do this he may pull or damage his muscles and find it difficult to concentrate.

Wind assisted: A performance which has been aided by a wind stronger than 2m/sec for individual events, or 4m/sec for heptathlon and decathlon.

Winding up: In order to help the discus and hammer gather speed, an athlete will carry out a few preliminary swings before beginnning to move across the circle.

Winding up the pace: A tactic used in long distance races in which the leader will steadily increase the race pace every 100m to 400m in order to tire his opponents.

Conversion table

Distances

10mm – 0.4in
500mm – 1ft 7in

1m – 3ft 3in
2m – 6ft 7in
3m – 9ft 10in
4m – 4yds 1ft 1in
5m – 5yds 1ft 5in
6m – 6yds 1ft 8in
7m – 7yds 1ft 11in
8m – 8yds 2ft 3in
9m – 9yds 2ft 6in
10m – 10yds 2ft 10in

20m – 21yds 2ft 8in
30m – 32yds 2ft 6in
40m – 43yds 2ft 3in
50m – 54yds 2ft 1in
60m – 65yds 1ft 11in
70m – 76yds 1ft 9in
80m – 87yds 1ft 7in
90m – 98yds 1ft 5in
100m – 109yds 1ft 2in

110m – 120yds 1ft
200m – 218yds 2ft 5in
300m – 328yds 7in

400m – 437yds 1ft 10in
500m – 547yds
600m – 656yds 1ft 2in
700m – 765yds 2ft 5in
800m – 875yds 7in
900m – 984yds 1ft 10in
1000m – 1094yds

1500m – 1641yds
1609m – 1 mile
3,000m – 1 mile 1522yds
5,000m – 3 miles 190yds
10,000m – 6 miles 376yds
42.195km – 26 miles 385yds

Weights

100gm – 4oz
500gm – 1lbs 2oz

1kg – 2lbs 3oz
2kg – 4lbs 6oz
3kg – 6lbs 10oz
4kg – 8lbs 13oz
5kg – 11lbs
6kg – 13lbs 3oz
7kg – 15lbs 6oz
8kg – 17lbs 10oz

Index